"Tell me about Arkansas."

By Tucker Steinmetz

With an Introduction by Governor Bill Clinton

A Commemorative Perspective on Arkansas
After One Hundred Fifty Years of Statehood

Published by Official Commission of

The State of Arkansas
Office of The Governor

Arkansas Sesquicentennial Commission
and
Department of Arkansas Heritage

Governor

Library of Congress Cataloging-in-Publication Data

Steinmetz, Tucker, 1941-
    Tell me about Arkansas.

    Includes index.
    1. Arkansas—Civilization.   2. Arkansas—Description
and travel—1981-   —Views.   3. Arkansas—Biography.
I. Title.
F411.S793   1988   976.7   88-6337
ISBN 0-944325-01-7 (pbk.)

There was a time when Arkansas was an isolated, quaint little place somewhere on the fringe of civilization, little known to the outside world and little interested in affairs beyond its borders.

That was the Arkansas that Thomas Nuttall and Henry Schoolcraft visited and wrote about in the early 19th Century: a beautiful, wild place populated by good, friendly, God-fearing folks who were desperately poor.

That characterization of our state was accurate for more than a hundred years after it was first recorded. Through the turn of this century, through the Depression and two World Wars, we persisted, proud but poor, living in a land rich in potential but with only pockets of prosperity.

Today, we live in an Arkansas that is greatly changed in several respects. We are not as poor as we were, nor as far behind. In fact, we have begun to lead other states in many ways. And we are no longer isolated. We are a state that is learning what it must do to become more than a quaint corner of the world, a state taking its first laborious steps toward becoming a part of the world economy.

This book tells the story of our journey—not just by reciting dates and facts, but by sharing the thoughts and words of Arkansans. In these pages you'll recognize your neighbors, your family and probably a little of yourself. You'll see and hear the spirit of the people who have brought Arkansas so far and who will take it proudly into the next century.

In 1986 we celebrated the Sesquicentennial of Arkansas statehood, a celebration this book commemorates. At that time we rededicated ourselves to the future, to the preservation of our natural beauty, the creativity of our people, our deeply-imbedded values and to the creation of the modern economic opportunities our people want, need and deserve.

To be true to that pledge, we have work to do. We must give our children a healthy start in life and build an education system that prepares them for a complex and very competitive world; we must maintain a competitive economic environment; we must lift the visibility of Arkansas so that anyone, anywhere, who can help our state on its way knows who we are, what we stand for and what we have to offer. And every community, every citizen in our state must be involved in the crafting of our destiny.

We don't have to do these things; if we don't, we'll still have what we've always had, what we had when Nuttall and Schoolcraft were here: our land, our values and our people. But we will never fulfill our potential, never quite achieve what our destiny could have been. We will never truly be a Land of Opportunity.

Our state takes its name from the great Arkansas River that flows from the Ozark foothills to the Mississippi delta. Imagine all the water that has rushed by on its way to the sea since our ancestors came here; imagine all the events that have occurred on that river's banks. History, like the river, flows but one way; we cannot reverse the current; but we can, without changing who we are, without losing what we hold dear, ride it to new adventures and better tomorrows.

Bill Clinton

Bill Clinton
Governor

Welcome to the last event in Arkansas's long celebration of 150 years of statehood.

This book, "Tell Me About Arkansas," is offered not as a glance backward over those years but as a perspective on the present and future of the nation's 36th state as it begins the next 150 years. We chose the title because we hope that as you open this book, you are saying to us, "Tell me about Arkansas."

Governor Clinton and the others who conceived this project envisioned a book which would introduce those outside our borders to the potential of Arkansas's future and convey to our young people a sense of pride in their origins and hope for the years ahead.

To achieve these goals, the book approaches its subject from three different vantage points, developed in three distinct sections, all aimed at telling you about Arkansas.

The first part of the book offers a perspective on a state poised for economic development in the coming decades. With its abundant natural resources and central location, its progressive government and concerned business community, Arkansas is preparing itself for a growing role in the national and international economies.

As the Twentieth Century nears its close, the entire world is experiencing economic changes occurring at an unprecedented rate. Arkansas, of course, has not been immune to these changes. We have had our share of factory closings and the inevitable ripple effects of the loss of jobs. Because of our traditional heavy reliance on agriculture, we have known intimately the tragic effects of what has come to be called the Farm Crisis of the 1980's.

But Arkansas has refused to despair.

All across the state, there are signs of hope. We offer "Perspective on Arkansas" as a sampling of the hopeful Arkansans on whom the future depends.

The second section of the book is a photographic essay designed to convey a warm impression of the natural beauty of Arkansas, its land and its people. This collection appeared originally in 1986, the Sesquicentennial year, as a book in itself. Widely circulated by the Office of the Governor and several state agencies, the book was well received at home and abroad.

(Incidentally, the people and places featured in the first two sections are in no way a thorough representation of Arkansas. There simply wasn't space to tell you about and show you all of the highlights of Arkansas. We didn't get to talk about Texarkana or Camden, Mountain Home or Jonesboro or scores of other delightful communities. With all of the beautiful color pictures, we still lacked a photograph of one of the Delta's oxbow lakes lined with tall, graceful cypress trees. There is a lot more to Arkansas. We hope we've told and shown enough here to get you to come and see for yourself.)

The third section of the book—"Sesquicentennial Sponsors"—presents photographs and profiles of 21 of the state's most valuable citizens, all well known here and most widely recognized far beyond the borders of Arkansas. Some are native Arkansans; others have adopted the state. All of them have chosen to base their business and civic activities in the state.

With a strong sense of obligation to the state in which they got their start, these Sesquicentennial Sponsors made possible through their generosity many of the events of Arkansas's celebration of its one hundred fiftieth birthday. The business enterprises led by these men and women affect the lives of thousands of Arkansans and many more Americans elsewhere. They are part of the backbone of the state's economy. Telling you about these unique individuals is one more way of telling you about Arkansas.

What Mr. Nuttall was trying to say, when these words fell onto his journal and obscured the message, was that Arkansas surely is a pretty place.

Fortunately for Arkansans, The Mamelle, now called Pinnacle Mountain, is not a volcano.

"*After emerging, as it were, from so vast a tract of alluvial lands, as that through which I had now been traveling for more than three months, it is almost impossible to describe the pleasure which these romantic prospects again afforded me. Who can be insensible to the beauty of the verdant hill and valley, to the sublimity of the clouded mountain, the fearful precipice, or the torrent of the cataract. Even bald and moss-grown rocks, without the aid of sculpture, forcibly inspire us with that veneration which we justly owe to the high antiquity of nature, and which appears to arise no less from a solemn and intuitive reflection on their vast capacity for duration, contrasted with that transient scene in which we ourselves only appear to act a momentary part.*"

--Thomas Nuttall, botanist near Little Rock, 1819

What Mr. Nuttall was trying to say, when these words fell onto his journal and obscured the message, was that Arkansas surely is a pretty place. When you consider where he was and what he was looking at, you can understand, and perhaps even pardon, his effusion of purple prose.

The self-taught English botanist had just experienced something the Arkansas geography offers in abundance: striking and strikingly beautiful contrasts of nature.

Nuttall had been slogging his way across the vast Delta of the Arkansas Territory and had reached the tiny settlement of Little Rock. Standing beside the Arkansas River, he could look back over his shoulder and see the river disappear into the far horizon flanked by seemingly endless flat bottomland. Looking ahead, Nuttall saw the hills alongside the Arkansas River west of Little Rock. He was particularly attracted to a conical mountain known in those days as The Mamelle [now spelled Maumelle], which looks for all the world like a volcano. Fortunately for Arkansans, The Mamelle, now called Pinnacle Mountain, is not a volcano. It is, though, a compelling sight, especially silhouetted against a sunset or shrouded in mists. Apparently sensing that his words might not suffice, Nuttall thoughtfully included in his journal an appealing sketch of The Mamelle.

The Englishman had reached what was to become the hub of Arkansas life. From this vantage point, he could, simply by climbing one of the nearby hills, get a fair sampling of the many landscapes of Arkansas. It was a land of water, mountains, rolling country and alluvial plain. Nuttall was at Little Rock, which became the territorial capital two years after his visit and, in 1836, became the capital of the new State of Arkansas. The botanist, by

Little Rock, named for a rock on the south bank of the Arkansas River, was little more than the rock and some 1,900 settlers, mostly rowdy frontiersmen.

Nuttall was more than a little chagrined by some of the rough and ready settlers in those early days.

the way, did not slight the Delta in the account of his journeys. Even in that early day, when East Arkansas was mostly swamps, dense forests, untamed prairies and lowlands subject to frequent flooding, he found it fertile and promising.

In 1819, when it was a new territory on the western frontier of a 43-year-old nation, Arkansas had maybe 14,000 inhabitants. Little Rock, named for a rock on the south bank of the Arkansas River, was little more than the rock and some 1,900 settlers, mostly rowdy frontiersmen. A year was to pass before the Reverend Cephas Washburn, a Presbyterian missionary to the Indians, would preach what he always contended was the first sermon ever heard in Little Rock.

The first territorial capital was at Arkansas Post near the confluence of the Arkansas and White Rivers just a few miles west of the Mississippi River. Other settlements were scattered mostly along streams navigable to small craft.

In Nuttall's day, the tremendous task of clearing the Delta was just beginning. The cypress swamps common to the eastern portion of the state were enlivened with snakes, alligators, king-sized mosquitoes and all the other creatures one would expect in such an environment. In

the rolling plains and the Ouachita Mountains of South and Central Arkansas were great expanses of virgin forests, mostly pine, dissected by a network of creeks, rivers and bayous. North of the Arkansas River Valley lay the Ozark Mountains, somewhat steeper and higher than the Ouachitas. In the undisturbed forests of the northern mountains, hardwoods, mainly oak and hickory, held sway.

One hundred fifty years of civilization quite naturally have left their mark on this 53,187 square miles in America's heartland. But, to the delight of more than two million Arkansans today, the years of settlement and development have only tended to shape and sculpt, not destroy, the state's rich and varied environment. While Thomas Nuttall and Cephas Washburn and all the other hearty souls who opened this land to western civilization would be at a loss to describe the Arkansas of today, they could not fail to recognize and delight in the enduring beauty of the landscape.

Nuttall was more than a little chagrined by some of the rough and ready settlers in those early days. Surely he would be pleased today to find a population noted for its warmth and friendliness.

Arkansas comprises 35 million acres that became the property of the United States with the Louisiana Purchase

The Delta brought the state its first significant wealth and gave Arkansas its only real claim to being part of the Old South.

in 1803. The diverse terrain, geologic features and plant life encompassed by the state's borders fall into six distinct natural divisions. They offer more variety of landscape than can be found in any other tract of similar size in America. The natural divisions are the Mississippi Alluvial Plain, the Ozark Mountains, the Arkansas River Valley, the Ouachita Mountains, the Gulf Coastal Plain and Crowley's Ridge.

Arkansans call the Mississippi Alluvial Plain the Delta. Covering about a third of the state, the Delta is a largely vertical expanse running from Missouri to Louisiana, with a bulging midline that sweeps westward to the outskirts of Little Rock. Smoothed and shaped thousands of years ago by the St. Francis, White, Ohio and Mississippi Rivers, it is a fertile region of deep, rich soils and abundant aquifers. In the early days of statehood, it was still heavily forested, largely with giant cypress trees rooted in wetlands.

Arkansas's recorded history is anchored in the east, where the early settlers crossed the Mississippi and located among the swamps and bayous. With axe and musket and grit, they extended the frontier beyond the bottomlands and prairies into the mountains, the Arkansas River Valley and

the rolling plains of South Arkansas. Many never left the Delta, however, choosing instead to put their roots down in a land that was transformed in just a few decades into a vast agricultural belt whose premier crop was cotton.

The Delta brought the state its first significant wealth and gave Arkansas its only real claim to being part of the Old South. The transition from dense, wet woodlands and wild prairies to a modern agricultural area has given the Delta a special beauty all its own. One sees it in the quiet, cypress-studded lakes or in lush fields of rice at harvest time.

Beginning up in Southeast Missouri and running southward from the northeast corner of Arkansas down to Helena, about midway between Missouri and Louisiana, is Crowley's Ridge. This scenic anomaly, made up primarily of clay and loess soils and gravel, rises as high as 250 feet above the Delta land around it.

It has become a picturesque setting for many small towns.

Geologists have haggled for decades over which of the Arkansas mountain ranges first reared up from the hot earth. Was it the Ozarks or the Ouachitas? It really doesn't matter. Both are be-

The Buffalo River, a pristine stream slicing through some of the most rugged stretches of the Ozarks, was the first official National River in the country.

Fifty million years ago, an ocean covered the south-central and southwest portions of Arkansas.

lieved to have emerged originally about 300 million years ago, subsequently wearing down, then being pushed up again by Nature's relentless pressures of creation. Long before it could have mattered to any of the forebears of present-day residents, both the Ozarks and the Ouachitas had mellowed to a soft beauty rivaling any other mountain range in the country.

The Arkansas Ozarks cover most of 21 counties across North Arkansas from the Oklahoma border on the west to within 50 miles of the Missouri Bootheel on the east. Comprising mostly sandstone, shale and limestone in horizontal layers, the Ozarks are heavily forested, with hardwoods predominant, and dissected by the clearest streams of every description. The Buffalo River, a pristine stream slicing through some of the most rugged stretches of the Ozarks, was the first official National River in the country.

The Ozarks are separated from the Ouachitas by the natural division known as the Arkansas River Valley, a broad, scenic expanse sweeping eastward from Fort Smith to northeast of North Little Rock, where it splays out into the Delta. The valley floor runs from about 500 to 600 feet above sea level, slowly rising toward the west. Enhancing its pastoral beauty are several mountains sitting like loaves on the valley floor. One of these, Magazine Mountain, tops out at 2,700 feet above sea level, the highest point in Arkansas.

The Ouachita Mountains lie south of the Arkansas River Valley, covering much of the southwestern quadrant of the state and part of Central Arkansas. These ridges of novaculite, sandstone, shale and chert harbor some of the state's least populated areas. Like the Ozarks, they are heavily forested and graced with rivers and creeks.

Fifty million years ago, an ocean covered the south-central and southwest portions of Arkansas. When the waters receded, they left the West Gulf Coastal Plain, a gently undulating land where the streams tend to be deeper and wider and to move slower than the noisy waters of the mountains.

The northern tip of the West Gulf Coastal Plain is just south of Little Rock, which again demonstrates the centrality of the capital city to the major natural divisions of the state. And that makes it central to the diverse cultures of the different regions of Arkansas. The earliest Arkansans couldn't have done better in selecting a site for their capital.

The Central Arkansas metropolitan area now has a population of about a half-

At the heart of downtown is a pedestrian mall, where a new $12.5 million complex of offices, boutiques and restaurants opened in 1987.

In contrast, Little Rock has, by careful design, preserved its Victorian heritage in a charming residential area south of downtown known as the Quapaw Quarter.

million people, yet it has managed to avoid the crowding and decay of the environment that so often accompany rapid urban growth.

Consider downtown Little Rock. It simply was never allowed to deteriorate. As the thriving city pushed its limits southward into the rolling plain and westward into the foothills of the Ouachitas, commerce followed, quite naturally. Modern malls were developed to serve the burgeoning residential populations in the growing new housing developments. It was a story repeated on the growing edges of many American cities, but Little Rock was determined to make its downtown an exception to what was becoming the national rule. Today, alongside the old buildings that have been lovingly restored and preserved are the new ones, tall and impressive tributes to the vitality of the city's financial and commercial interests. At the heart of downtown is a pedestrian mall, where a new $12.5 million complex of offices, boutiques and restaurants opened in 1987. To improve accessibility, business and city government have cooperated to provide ample and inexpensive downtown parking. And two freeways intersect just south of the downtown area to make it easy to enter and leave.

Many of the nation's larger cities have allowed once proud residential areas

to rot and finally turn into commercial or warehouse districts. In contrast, Little Rock has, by careful design, preserved its Victorian heritage in a charming residential area south of downtown known as the Quapaw Quarter.

Besides being a financial, commercial and distribution center for the state, Little Rock is home to some of the major educational institutions.

The University of Arkansas at Little Rock, once a private college, is now part of the University of Arkansas System, which is based at Fayetteville and has other campuses at Monticello and Pine Bluff. With an enrollment of nearly 10,000, UALR is meeting the unique needs of an urban area by offering classes on and off campus from early morning to late evening with both undergraduate and graduate programs.

The University System has two law schools. The older institution is located in Fayetteville. The UALR School of Law is in a downtown building within walking distance of federal and county courts and government offices and just a short drive from the Arkansas Court of Appeals, the Arkansas Supreme Court and the State Capitol. Its location enables the law school to involve some of Arkansas's finest lawyers in its program.

Today, UAMS graduates are distinguishing themselves in post-graduate programs throughout the United States.

Probably the accomplishment at UAMS best known and appreciated by the citizens of Arkansas is the dramatic increase in the training of specialists in family medicine.

Arkansas has always been proud of its medical school, but over the last two decades, the state has pursued a campaign to make the University of Arkansas for Medical Sciences one of the nation's most outstanding institutions in training and education, research and patient care. Today, UAMS graduates are distinguishing themselves in post-graduate programs throughout the United States.

In addition to its primary mission of training health-care personnel for the state, UAMS sees itself as a major contributor to economic growth in the very near future. The story of the spectacular development of UAMS since 1970 and the plans for its future merit more attention here.

Dr. Harry N. Ward, Chancellor of UAMS since 1979, is unabashedly proud of the school.

For six consecutive years, UAMS Medical School graduates have scored either first or second nationally in the Federal Licensing Examination, a rigorous test of medical education. This stellar performance has enabled UAMS graduates to gain admission to internships and residency training programs in the nation's finest teaching hospitals.

Probably the accomplishment at UAMS best known and appreciated by the citizens of Arkansas is

the dramatic increase in the training of specialists in family medicine. The origins of this highly successful program go back to 1971, when the State Legislature recognized that without a special and costly effort, the small towns of Arkansas could eventually find themselves in dire need of more primary-care physicians.

In response to the need, the Legislature approved funds to expand the family medicine program. Six Area Health Education Centers, satellites of UAMS, were established around the state to provide care and training. Financial incentives were developed to encourage more graduates to stay in Arkansas. From a humble beginning of six residency positions in family medicine, the program has grown to offer 104 positions.

These advances in medical training evolved as more small and medium-sized towns in Arkansas were experiencing economic development and other improvements. These factors combined to make life and medical practice in Arkansas more appealing to UAMS graduates. Whereas, prior to 1971 about 80 per cent of the UAMS Medical School graduates left the state, today about 70 per cent of them remain in the state. And physicians coming in from other states more than offset the 30 per cent who leave.

13

The icing on this cake is the fact that increasing numbers of medical specialists are opting for at least part-time practice in smaller towns and communities.

This dramatic increase in the number and competency of family physicians in the state, coupled with the impressive growth and development of regional hospitals, has removed one of the major impediments to economic development outside urban areas in Arkansas.

The icing on this cake is the fact that increasing numbers of medical specialists are opting for at least part-time practice in smaller towns and communities.

The economic potential for private medically-related business development in the Little Rock metropolitan area will increase markedly in the next few years as UAMS completes its regional cancer research and treatment center and a new research building. These new facilities and joint ventures with the National Center for Toxicological Research just south of Little Rock will make UAMS a major actor in the development of the planned high-technology corridor between Little Rock and Pine Bluff.

The training and treatment capabilities of UAMS are greatly enhanced by cooperation with neighboring institutions. Instead of treating children at University Hospital, the school has made the Arkansas Children's Hospital, one of the state's most venerable private institutions, its official Pediatrics Department. The marriage of these institutions has been highly beneficial for both. Children's Hospital, just a short drive down Interstate 630 from UAMS, has a national reputation and a beautiful and modern facility. The hospital attracts the generous donations of some of Arkansas's most prominent philanthropists as well as wide general support around the state. The other institution associated with UAMS is the new John L. McClellan Memorial Veterans Administration Hospital on the UAMS campus. The Medical School is responsible for professional staffing at the ultra-modern VA Hospital.

University Hospital, the base of the UAMS programs, attracts a clientele that cuts broadly across socio-economic lines in Arkansas. Private-pay patients now account for half the patient load in the teaching hospital, and the money generated by these patients has been used to renovate the facility.

Dr. Ward sees sound, meaningful research as indispensable to sound, meaningful medical training. Consequently, UAMS has set out to excel in four broad areas of research: geriatrics, toxicology, neuro-muscular and muscular-skeletal diseases, and cancer.

Outside funding for research at UAMS is soaring, going from about $4 million

The Arkansas Symphony, in its 21-year history, has matured into a musical organization with a roster of 80 professional players and a varied program that brings live performances to thousands annually.

in 1986 to $7.9 million in 1987. Dr. Ward wants it at a level of $12 to $14 million annually.

Ground has been broken for a cancer center comparable to the Lurleen Wallace Cancer Center at Birmingham, Alabama. Designation as a regional cancer center will qualify it for vastly increased federal funding. Dr. Ward likes to point out that at least six private companies in the medical field moved to Birmingham because of the center. He sees no reason why that story couldn't be repeated in Arkansas.

Dr. Ward, a native of Colorado, is a magna cum laude graduate of Princeton University, where he majored in biology and minored in English literature. He earned his medical degree from the University of Colorado School of Medicine and did an internship at New York's Bellevue Hospital before undertaking a residency in hematology at the Mayo Clinic in Rochester, Minnesota. He is a recognized expert on agnogenic myeloid metaplasia, a form of leukemia.

He came to UAMS from the Colorado School of Medicine, where he was the dean.

For the Wards, life in Little Rock is good. They have been active supporters of the Arkansas Symphony,

the United Way, the Arkansas Repertory Theatre, the public schools and the Arkansas Opera Theater.

A look at some of the features of Arkansas life that have appealed to the Wards demonstrates why so many residents of other states have moved here and put down permanent roots.

Consider the fine arts and the humanities, for example.

The Arkansas Symphony, in its 21-year history, has matured into a musical organization with a roster of 80 professional players and a varied program that brings live performances to thousands annually. The Robinson Auditorium at the Little Rock Convention Center is packed for the Symphony's classical and pop concerts. The 55-member Touring Orchestra presents 12 classical and three pop concerts each season. In addition, the Symphony's 32-member Chamber Orchestra makes ten to 12 appearances around the state each season, and the four full-time musicians of the String Quartet perform almost continually all across Arkansas. During a single season, the Quartet will play for about 50,000 school children in 125 demonstrations.

Each year the Symphony brings to Arkansas outstanding soloists like Leontyne Price, Van Cliburn or Itzhak Perlman.

The Opera also operates one of the largest touring programs for the public schools in the United States, bringing live opera to an estimated 47,000 Arkansas students every year.

In 1976 a group of Arkansans decided the state was ready for a professional theater of its own.

The Symphony enjoys broad popular support that has enabled it to expand its budget from a modest $54,000 in 1970 to more than $800,000 in 1987.

The success of the Little Rock-based Orchestra has encouraged the continuing success of five smaller symphonies around the state at Pine Bluff, El Dorado, Jonesboro, Fayetteville and Fort Smith.

In addition to their service in the regular performances of the Symphony, the Orchestra members provide the musical support for the Arkansas Opera Theatre, a 15-year-old organization offering four Mainstage opera productions and two Cabaret Dinner Theater presentations annually. The Opera also operates one of the largest touring programs for the public schools in the United States, bringing live opera to an estimated 47,000 Arkansas students every year.

In 1987 the Opera began planning the first stage of a $17.4 million complex for the performing arts on a scenic 92-acre site in the hills west of Little Rock. Scheduled for completion by the fall of 1989 are a 700-seat theater with orchestra pit, a Village on the Green for outdoor festival performances and a 10,000-seat outdoor amphitheater. The entire complex will be the largest project for the arts in the

history of Arkansas.

Theater has always been popular here. Stage presentations have long been offered by the public schools, universities and community theater groups. For many years, touring professionals from Broadway and elsewhere have played to sell-out crowds in Little Rock. In 1976 a group of Arkansans decided the state was ready for a professional theater of its own. They formed the Arkansas Repertory Theatre and managed a budget of about $50,000 the first year. In 1987, The Rep, as it has come to be known, played to sell-out crowds, had a budget of more than $830,000 and undertook an ambitious building program to give Arkansas one of the finest theater centers in the South.

The Rep has simply outgrown its 140-seat theater in a former church building near Little Rock's MacArthur Park. Every year more performances have sold out; the full-time staff has grown, and a statewide educational program has expanded. Not only would the theater not accommodate all who wanted to attend, but it could not generate the income needed to support such a broad program. In 1987 The Rep expanded its usual four-week runs to five weeks for each main production. When all of its MainStage and Second-Stage productions are added to The Rep's Arts-In-Educa-

The Arts Center spent more than $2.2 million in fiscal 1987 in its broad program touching the lives of some 100,000 Arkansans statewide.

In 1985 the Center opened the Decorative Arts Museum in the Pike-Terry-Fletcher House, considered by many historians to be the most significant house in Arkansas today.

tion appearances, the organization will have presented more than 300 performances in the 1987-88 season.

Early in 1987, The Rep purchased the Galloway Building, a landmark on Main Street in downtown Little Rock, and began extensive restoration and remodeling. It is scheduled to open in the fall of 1988.

Not far away to the east, nestled in the quiet beauty of MacArthur Park (birthplace of General Douglas MacArthur), is the Arkansas Arts Center—an art museum, a teaching institution and a center for the performing arts. Opened in 1963 with an operating budget of $835,000, the Arts Center spent more than $2.2 million in fiscal 1987 in its broad program touching the lives of some 100,000 Arkansans statewide. The Center is supported by state and local government contributions, corporate giving, membership dues and a growing endowment fund that now exceeds $7.5 million.

Continuous exhibitions at the Center come from the Arkansas Arts Center Foundation Collection, the works of the Center's faculty and other Arkansas artists and from traveling exhibitions organized by major museums and exhibition services.

In 1985 the Center opened the Decorative Arts Museum in the Pike-Terry-

Fletcher House, considered by many historians to be the most significant house in Arkansas today. Built in 1840, the mansion was home to some of the state's most prominent citizens, from politicians to literary figures, until 1977, when it was deeded to the City of Little Rock for use by the Arts Center.

The Center's Department of Education offers classes to students of all ages in art, dance and theater. In fiscal 1987 the school experienced a 50% increase in enrollment to 2,227 students.

In a reappraisal of the art collection, Sotheby's determined that the value of the works had increased from $3.7 million in 1981 to $7.8 million in 1987.

Making the enjoyment of all the arts widely available around the state, in addition to providing in-depth information services and educational programming, are public broadcasting media—the Arkansas Educational Television Network and four public radio stations affiliated with National Public Radio, KLRE-FM and KUAR-FM, both of Little Rock; KASU, operated by Arkansas State University at Jonesboro, and KUAF, operated by the University of Arkansas at Fayetteville.

AETN started as a one-station operation in 1966 and added four stations in

One of the most significant features of all the major cultural institutions of Central Arkansas is that each has an aggressive outreach effort to take its artistic offerings out into the state.

the late 1970's to provide coverage for the entire state. Over the years, the station has become immensely popular and enjoyed increasing public support. The General Assembly appropriates basic operating funds for the station and underwrites the daytime educational programs aimed primarily at the public schools. In order to offer prime-time programs, including nationally produced documentaries, features and news, the station has two annual on-the-air fund-raising events. About 30,000 Arkansans are contributors.

AETN's total budget exceeds $6 million a year.

KLRE-FM began a very limited operation in 1972 under the auspices of the Little Rock School District, starting out with only 45 hours a week of daytime programming with a monaural signal and only 3,600 watts of power. Today, thanks to steadily increasing public support, the station is on the air 24 hours a day with 40,000 watts of power and a stereophonic signal. It is a National Public Radio affiliate and broadcasts "All Things Considered" and other nationally acclaimed public radio programs. The station's major program fare is classical music supplemented with jazz and folk music and information programs drawing on the resources of the Little Rock School District and the University of Arkan-

sas at Little Rock.

KLRE and KUAR, which is licensed to the University, are now simulcasting, which reaches a broader audience due to KUAR's 100,000-watt transmitter. Eventually, the stations expect to have separate programming.

One of the most significant features of all the major cultural institutions of Central Arkansas is that each has an aggressive outreach effort to take its artistic offerings out into the state.

Besides its broad offerings in the fine arts, Arkansas has maintained a consuming interest in history and preservation of the artifacts of its heritage. The state has almost 100 active, full-fledged museums that own their own collections, have a staff and engage in exhibition, interpretation, research and preservation. That's quite an accomplishment for a state with a population of just over 2 million.

The two largest university museums are at the University of Arkansas at Fayetteville and Arkansas State University at Jonesboro. Among the other outstanding facilities are the Museum of Science and History in MacArthur Park at Little Rock, which focuses on natural and cultural history of the state and has an impressive North American Indian collection; the Old

State House, a splendid structure on the south bank of the Arkansas River at Little Rock, the state's first Capitol and the home of a growing collection of material depicting Arkansas's history since 1836, and the Arkansas Territorial Restoration near downtown Little Rock, a collection of historical houses and early government buildings from the Territorial Period (1819-1836).

Just outside Hot Springs is the Mid-America Museum, which features science and technology and demonstrates principles of physics with hands-on exhibits. Smackover is the site of the first phase of the Oil and Brine Museum, which has outdoor exhibits illustrating primarily pumping technology from 1920 to the present. In 1988, the Oil and Brine Museum will open a 26,000-square-foot building with exhibits focusing on the historical, cultural and technological aspects of the oil boom that changed South Arkansas in the 1920's.

Not any area of the state is without at least a scattering of good museums and historic buildings open to the public.

The artistic interests of Arkansans are certainly not limited to the fine arts, and a visitor to the state quickly discovers that creative expression is endemic to the Arkansas way of life.

Talented native crafters are so numerous and competent here that many giftware manufacturers don't bother to send sales representatives to Arkansas. The state's artisans have a national reputation for making their own gifts and decorative accessories. And just when it appears that some old craft technique is about to vanish forever, it will enjoy a startling resurgence. Quilting, for example, appeared not too many years ago to be on the wane. It seemed that the old-fashioned quilting bee would linger only in memory and in the works of primitive painters. Today, fine quilts are in demand, and fine quilters are responding to the market. Their products reveal that this old art form has lost none of its vitality at the hands of its latter-day practitioners.

Several major shows around the state annually display the handmade works of Arkansas's artists and crafters.

Music is part of the Arkansas soul, not just the music from the instruments of the professionals, but homespun fare. The Ozark Mountains have a proud tradition of folk music, which is being kept alive by native musicians of today. The Rackensack Society, based in Little Rock, is devoted to the preservation of this type of music and offers a generous feast of it at its monthly

Just outside Hot Springs is the Mid-America Museum, which features science and technology and demonstrates principles of physics with hands-on exhibits.

The annual Folk Festival at Mountain View consistently draws crowds from all over the United States.

Clean water is so abundant in Arkansas that at least one neighboring state has tried to figure out a way to tap the supply.

meetings at the Arkansas Arts Center. Perhaps the greatest concentration of folk musicians is at Mountain View, up in Stone County, home of the Ozark Folk Center. Many Mountain View residents moved there simply because of the music. On just about any night of the week, guitar pickers, dulcimer strummers, banjo players, singers, fiddlers and all the other elements of mountain music can be heard on the courthouse lawn or any one of several street corners and porches downtown.

The annual Folk Festival at Mountain View consistently draws crowds from all over the United States.

The culture and beauty of the Ozarks alone would be sufficient to make Arkansas a major tourist state. When you add to those attractions the almost limitless recreational opportunities, it is not surprising to learn that millions of visitors come to Arkansas every year to spend part of their leisure time. Those who keep track of such matters reckon that the economic impact of travel and tourism in Arkansas in 1986 amounted to more than $1.9 billion.

Much of the attention centers around water—vast, beautiful stretches of surface water, more than 1,100 square miles of it, including 33 major lakes scattered around the state, more than 800 natural oxbow and cut-off lakes and more than 9,000

miles of streams worth fishing. The number of fishing licenses sold annually is staggering. In fiscal 1987, the state Game and Fish Commission sold 431,744 resident fishing licenses and another 76,918 non-resident licenses good for the year. In addition to those, the agency sold 128,301 three-day licenses to Arkansans and residents of other states.

Clean water is so abundant in Arkansas that at least one neighboring state has tried to figure out a way to tap the supply. Clearly, this resource is a benefit to economic development. Beyond that, Arkansans put it to about every recreational use imaginable. You won't find ice skating (the winters here aren't hard enough for that), surfing or deep-sea fishing, but you can swim, water ski, scuba dive, ride the wind in a sailboat or on a sailboard, fish, go white-water canoeing or even dive for rare pearls found in mussel shells.

Many of the earliest settlers in Arkansas were hunters; hunting remains a hallowed tradition. Arkansas citizens purchased nearly 197,081 hunting licenses in the fiscal year ended July 31, 1987, and 25,903 hunters from other states purchased nonresident licenses. They descended on the state's waterways, fields and forests to hunt ducks, squirrels, rabbits, turtle doves, turkey, geese, quail, raccoons, black

Many out-of-state visitors and residents who want to enjoy the outdoors flock to Arkansas's 44 well-run state parks.

The ultimate sporting event in Arkansas is a Razorback football game.

bears, wild hogs and deer, all available in abundance due to sound wildlife management and excellent habitat. While most hunters use modern shotguns and rifles, more and more Arkansans are developing a knack for hunting with bows and muzzle-loaders.

Many out-of-state visitors and residents who want to enjoy the outdoors flock to Arkansas's 44 well-run state parks. They're evenly spread around the state to make inexpensive camping or day trips in clean, family-oriented environments readily available to everyone. These parks are supplemented by camping areas operated by the National Park Service, the U.S. Forest Service and the U.S. Army Corps of Engineers.

In addition to ardent devotion to outdoor recreation, Arkansans have a long-standing love affair with team sports, both as spectators and participants.

By the time a town has a few hundred residents, it is going to have a ballfield. Let it top a thousand inhabitants, and the field is part of a complex, and it is lighted and has bleachers. Little children, just getting started in school, get some of their earliest training in teamwork playing softball. Later, they can get into touch football and basketball or soccer.

Church leagues for softball and baseball abound.

Theological differences are put aside for a few nights a week during ball season while the more agile believers match wits and brawn under the lights.

School sports become rallying points for communities. Junior and senior high sporting events are heavily attended.

The ultimate sporting event in Arkansas is a Razorback football game. The team of the University of Arkansas at Fayetteville has done so well over the years that it may be one of the things for which Arkansas is best known. Hundreds of Arkansas businesses use Razorback in their names, and manufacturers have turned out every imaginable kind of Razorback memorabilia from barbecue grills to hardhats.

In the last few years, the Indians of Arkansas State University at Jonesboro have improved their performances on the football field to the point that Indian partisans are calling for an annual match with the Razorbacks.

Stronger basketball teams at the UA campuses at Fayetteville and Little Rock and at Arkansas State have stirred unprecedented interest in that sport. All three teams frequently play to sell-out crowds. In the spring of 1987, all three participated in the National Invitational Tournament, in which UAF and ASU finally met for the

The General Assembly has imposed tough new standards on the public schools, including a controversial re-testing of all certified personnel, broader course offerings and more stringent standards for graduation.

The Arkansas Industry Training Program is rated as one of the best efforts of its kind in the United States.

first time in a sporting event.

In recent years, the UAF Track Team has been gaining prominence. By 1987 it was recognized as the most outstanding track team in the United States.

The state's smaller universities and colleges have distinguished themselves in sports, too. The University of Central Arkansas at Conway, for example, the Arkansas Intercollegiate Conference football champions for five years now, shared national championships in 1984 and 1985. The men's basketball team from the University of Arkansas at Monticello made it to the NAIA national finals in 1986. The women's basketball team from Arkansas Tech University at Russellville reached the finals in 1987.

While an agreeable environment, availability of the arts and a wide range of recreational activities are vital ingredients of the quality of Arkansas life, they are not the only ones. Educational opportunity enjoys a high priority.

The General Assembly has imposed tough new standards on the public schools, including a controversial re-testing of all certified personnel, broader course offerings and more stringent standards for graduation. A one-cent sales tax was approved to fund the improvements. The public response

to this effort has been heartening. The voters of some districts approved drastic increases in school taxes to meet the standards.

Arkansas has 20 state-supported and 12 independent institutions of higher education offering undergraduate work in all fields within easy driving distance of just about every citizen. Several institutions offer graduate degrees.

Vocational education classes are available in more than 300 high schools around the state, and a network of post-secondary vocational-technical schools offers training in more than 50 fields.

The Arkansas Industry Training Program is rated as one of the best efforts of its kind in the United States. Projects undertaken by the program are designed to meet the particular needs of each participating company by preparing trainees to go directly to work in new or expanded manufacturing plants.

All of this bodes well for the future of Arkansas. The ingredients of the good life are here, and the business climate is excellent.

There is a movement underway in many of the smaller towns of Arkansas, an effort growing out of an awareness that indifference to economic reality inevitably leads to decline. Many communities have learned through bitter experience that an industrial base cannot be taken for granted, that to assume a factory, once operating, will always be there is to court disaster. While any area of the state would extend a welcome to a big new employer, community leaders are facing the fact that the majority of new jobs come from small and medium-sized businesses. They are also learning that the cultivation of new enterprises and the expansion of old require sustained, organized community effort.

Ernest Whitelaw, a community development counselor for Arkansas Power & Light Company, is unreservedly enthusiastic about the future of the state. He says:

"I've seen more change in Arkansas within the last year than I've seen in a long time. It's as though the leaders of the communities are waking up and realizing that if they're ever going to do anything, they're going to have to do it for themselves."

Much of this rather dramatic awakening is probably attributable to the strengthening of the programs of the Arkansas Industrial Development Commission (AIDC). In the past, when it was not as well funded, the AIDC had to concentrate most of its efforts on the recruitment of larger com-

panies from outside the state. Today, the agency continues the search for the big plants but commits more of its resources to helping communities identify their strengths, rectify their weaknesses and present themselves well to industrial prospects. Two new AIDC programs—Cross-Match and Matchmaker—are designed to get Arkansas businesses buying from each other. The aim is to reduce the purchase of components and materials from outside the state.

AIDC staff members cover the entire state offering training and consultation to cities and small towns eager to strengthen their economic base. To supplement and formalize this training, the University of Central Arkansas at Conway, a state-supported institution, has established a continuing-education program for community developers—local residents who want to make a significant contribution to their hometown's wellbeing. The University hopes to become a national center for training community developers.

There are enough stories of outstanding individual and community efforts around Arkansas these days to fill volumes. A few examples have been selected for presentation here.

First—to the Delta.

Driving northeast out

of North Little Rock on U.S. Highway 67-167 takes the traveler over the rolling transitional ground between the uppermost reaches of the Ouachita Mountains and the Delta. Off to the east is open farm country that goes all the way to the Mississippi River.

In the 1980's, the farmer has had a lot to get him down. Farm commodity prices went into a slide early in the decade, some of them bottoming out at 20-year lows. Land prices, after soaring to dizzying heights, plummeted and left many with mortgages much larger than the depressed value of the land. One result has been a shaking out of more tenuous operations.

At several locations in the Delta one finds giant mounds of rice sheathed in plastic. Just outside Augusta, in the summer of 1987, were four of these vacuum-packed bags, each containing about 600,000 bushels of surplus rice being held by the federal government. Just down the road were rice fields, where production went on in the shadow of surplus.

The equipment yards at farm-implement dealerships reflect the changing times. Parts and service are a bigger share of the business now. You don't see many new pieces out front. There is a nice market for used machinery.

He could have gone the way of many dealers and folded his tents and looked for another means of livelihood. He chose to tough it out.

Charles Eldredge at Augusta has been in the implement business all his working life. It is a family tradition. Sales were booming in the 1970's. Tractors were getting bigger and better. Times were good. When agriculture took a dive in this decade, Eldredge's business declined along with that of his customers. He could have gone the way of many dealers and folded his tents and looked for another means of livelihood. He chose to tough it out. One day he sold a badly burned tractor to a salvage dealer in another state. A hasty calculation of what he got for the supposed junk and what the other man would probably expect to make off of it intrigued Eldredge. After another salvage deal, he began to reconsider his future.

Today, most of the seven-acre site of his dealership is covered with used tractors and implements. To the casual observer, it appears to be a field of rusting and useless steel. To Eldredge, it is a gold mine. That old combine you see may never ply the bean rows again. But its drive shaft or starter or some other vital part will have a new life in another combine that some struggling farmer is nursing along until times get better.

Eldredge has got into the salvage business in a big way. He buys and sells all over the United States.

"You hate to be defeated," he says. "You stay there until the last lick is passed."

Does he even think about quitting?

"It always runs across your mind. You think about a lot of things. But mostly, you think about how to combat the problem."

And how is that?

"Just keep on working."

Down below Augusta, in the southern part of Woodruff County, is the town of Cotton Plant, home of Harrison Locke, a man devoted to farming who refuses to surrender to hard times. Like Eldredge he has come to appreciate old tractors and plows.

"You hate to be defeated," he says. "You stay there until the last lick is passed."

Does he even think about quitting?

"It always runs across your mind. You think about a lot of things. But mostly, you think about how to combat the problem."

And how is that?

"Just keep on working."

Locke smiles. He's not about to leave. Besides, things looked a little better by mid-1987. Prudent management had brought him through the worst of the crisis.

Locke is 57 years old. His grandfather acquired part of the land Locke still farms today. His father, now 83 and mostly retired, spent all his active years on the farm.

As a young man, Locke earned a degree in agricultural education at the University of Arkansas at Pine Bluff and started teaching in a program for veterans at Marvell. He transferred to the Forrest City schools in 1957, back when that district had a split term to accommodate planting and harvest seasons. Agriculture teachers taught year around. But with the break provided by the split term and a two-week vacation, Locke was able to plant and harvest 50 acres of soybeans annually. He would make from $10,000 to $15,000 on the beans and less than $4,000 teaching. Finally overwhelmed by both the mathematics of his incomes and the lure of the soil, Locke left the classroom in 1962 and went home to be a full-time farmer. He has never looked back.

The farm has grown from just a few more than 200 acres to about 1,000 acres today. He owns 460 acres and rents the rest.

Locke's equipment yard sprawls along the edge of a bean field several miles out of town. Most of the paint is gone from the rusted finishes on tractors, plows, combines and a cotton picker. But except for the cotton picker (he gave up cotton several years ago), the equipment is still used every year. Locke can do about any kind of repair work. That's good because he doesn't buy new implements these days. His four big tractors have been in service for years.

Some of the machinery sat under a long shed at the

"Someone has got to stay," Locke says. "Everybody cannot just jump up and run off."

The last time he was quoted in print calling for a free farm market, Stanley says, he "caught some flack" from peers who disagreed.

back of the lot until 1986, when a tornado destroyed half of the building. In the spring of 1987, another tornado came through and took out what was left. The equipment was spared. Locke can get by without the building. So he can laugh about the story.

Locke expects better days ahead.

"Someone has got to stay," Locke says. "Everybody cannot just jump up and run off."

Farming clearly suffered some setbacks in this decade, but the tenacity of men like Harrison Locke assures that agriculture will remain a vital force in the Arkansas economy.

Back up near Augusta, in the rich bottomland between the White and the Cache Rivers, are two other farmers unwilling to give up. David Stanley of Augusta and Jim Burton of Newport are seeking better ways to live off the land. They are part of a vanguard of innovative farmers who intend to stay in the fields but put the land to new uses.

Stanley is an intense, introspective young farmer who would rather see the federal government out of agriculture, although he entertains no notions of that ever happening. The last time he was quoted in print calling for a free farm market,

Stanley says, he "caught some flack" from peers who disagreed.

When Stanley settled down to farming with his father in 1975, the outlook for expanding markets was good. A common scenario promoted by the prognosticators of the day was that oil-fueled Third World economies would create immense demand for American farm produce. In 1980, Stanley expanded his operation to make it more productive and efficient, taking full advantage of the explosion in agricultural technology and chemistry. He acquired more land and was poised to take full advantage of those new markets. They didn't materialize.

A year later, inflation cooled, oil prices declined, the value of the dollar rose, and the Third World was left awash in debts it couldn't repay. Stanley had a highly efficient 4,000-acre farm, the very kind of operation he is convinced the 1981 federal farm program did not help. Only in 1987 did hopeful signs appear. The "darkest hour" has passed for now, Stanley believes. He is not ready to give up on conventional agriculture. However, he is unwilling to continue a total reliance on traditional East Arkansas farming, knowing instinctively that bad times will return as part of the endless cycles of the agricultural economy.

"One thing about the fresh market," Burton says, "it doesn't make a damn what the exchange rate (of dollars) is, and you're competing with American farmers."

"I want to find something that I can sell to the public at a nice price and make some money," Stanley said in mid-1987.

At this point in a long conversation about farming, Stanley brightened. He was noticeably more animated. After lunch in a grove of hardwoods behind his house, he drove his visitors out to near Tupelo to show what he was so excited about.

Just about a mile south of Tupelo is where Jim Burton has built his vegetable shed, a high metal building with a massive refrigerated locker, a hydro-cooler, offices and two pieces of processing equipment you won't find anywhere else in Arkansas.

Burton, an engineer by education, has a 3,000-acre conventional farm outside of Tupelo. His grandfather started the farm. Like Stanley, Burton has a fiercely independent streak about him. He is weary of trying to figure out how to make a living working the government farm programs.

Burton thinks he is onto something promising: sweet corn for the wholesale fresh market in about a third of the United States, cucumbers for the Atkins Pickle Company in West Arkansas and, eventually, other vegetables in mass quantities.

"One thing about the fresh market," Burton says, "it doesn't make a damn what the exchange rate (of dollars) is, and you're competing with American farmers."

You can put a dollar value on just how serious Burton is about this venture in vegetables. He has invested about a half-million dollars in the shed and its equipment.

Green Bay Foods, Inc., which now owns Atkins Pickle, has a smaller, but certainly significant, stake in Burton's experiment. The Wisconsin-based company has stationed a $100,000 Dutch-made cucumber grader at Burton's shed. A crew from The Netherlands installed the grader in May 1987.

To assure a reasonable supply of cucumbers, Burton invited Stanley to participate. Stanley committed 150 acres to the project to match Burton's 150 acres. Burton purchased two automatic cucumber harvesters and mounted them on four-wheel drive tractors dedicated to the pickle project. Atkins committed to taking everything the farmers could raise in two plantings in 1987.

In order to give more attention to the project, Burton got someone to farm his rice acreage, and Stanley took on a partner, Joe Neal, for his cucumber acreage. Neal is a college-educated agronomist with a nose for

Neal is a college-educated agronomist with a nose for adventure. He spent several years in Colorado as a ski patrolman.

Burton designed and built the corn-grading contraption himself.

adventure. He spent several years in Colorado as a ski patrolman.

Burton estimated that by the time the shed fell silent in late September 1987, he would process 90,000 crates of fancy-grade sweet corn and 100,000 bushels of cucumbers.

The corn is coming off 300 acres on Burton's farm. He has had no trouble selling it, mostly to supermarket chains from Florida to North Dakota.

In late June 1987, the vegetable shed was in full operation with about 70 people working in two shifts to handle the corn and cucumbers.

Most of them were processing corn, which was brought from the fields and dumped onto a conveyor belt that lifted it above a row of wire bins. A young man in the control booth guided the gates that directed the corn into the bins, where workers picked up the fancy corn and placed it in crates. They threw everything else onto a lower conveyor which moved past two women who were removing Number One grade corn and placing it in large bins. What was left after that, the roughest ears and some leaves, was lifted by another conveyor and dumped into waiting pickups. People came from miles around to buy these leftovers in bulk.

Burton designed and built the corn-grading contraption himself.

The cucumbers were dumped into a vat of turbulent water, which knocked most of the dirt off of them. A conveyor then carried them past eight workers who removed the damaged or imperfect cucumbers. From there, the cucumbers were lifted up to an ingenious but strikingly simple device which dropped them into waiting bins in six different sizes. This section of the grader consists of a series of chains covered with plastic links. The distance between the chains gradually increases. The smallest cucumbers fall out first. Those that are too big to be Atkins Pickles ride high until they go over the end of the conveyor into a waste bin.

Both corn and cucumbers must be cooled down quickly to preserve freshness. A forklift scoops up pallets of corn crates and bins of cucumbers and slides them into the hydro-cooler, a rectangular outfit which douses the produce with 36-degree water. (The cooler was manufactured by the Clarksville, Arkansas, Machine Works.) Cucumbers are cooled to under 50 degrees and corn to less than 45 degrees. At the other end of the tunnel, the vegetables are moved into the 38-degree locker to await transport in refrigerated vans.

Raising a cucumber crop is quick, taking only about 42 days, and tricky, being vulnerable to ill-timed rains, disease and farmer mistakes. At about 32 days, the first yellow blooms appear. Bees from the rented hives in the field quickly pollinate these, and in ten days the first cucumber on each vine is expected to be one of the six sizes Atkins Pickle will buy. It will be growing a size a day. The harvest must be completed in about two days. Delay beyond that leaves too many oversized cucumbers. A heavy rain at the critical moment can keep the ponderous mechanical harvesters out of the field. Rain can also rot the bottoms of the cucumbers.

The frequent rains in June of 1987 played havoc with the harvesting of the first crops, but the yield was still good.

Burton, Stanley and Neal will have a bigger crop in 1988. Burton says that Atkins Pickle imported 2,500 acres of cucumbers in 1986 during the Arkansas growing season. He would like to grow a good portion of those himself.

What Burton and Stanley hope for is the gradual introduction of other vegetable crops that haven't been grown in Arkansas on a large-scale basis. For several years, Stanley has been experimenting with small plots of other vegetables. In 1987 he successfully tested broccoli, a hot item nowadays in the American market.

"We can be another California," Stanley contends. "I don't have a doubt in my mind."

In the middle of the cucumber and corn harvest in June, Burton was a study in perpetual motion. One morning he was out front trying to start the refrigeration unit on a van. The locker was filling up fast, and he needed to spill some of it over into the van. Before he got the unit running, Burton was called out to Stanley's farm to fix a brake line on one of his trucks that was hauling cucumbers. With 70 people on the payroll and perishable produce ready in the fields, he couldn't afford a break in the production chain. All the while he kept an eye on the dark clouds coming out of the west.

Is he glad he got into this venture?

"It's much better than sitting around fretting," he answered. "I don't have time to get depressed."

Burton doesn't give much thought to the possibility of failure. He drives himself with this philosophy:

"There are two kinds of people—those that think they can and those that think

> "There are two kinds of people—those that think they can and those that think they can't. Both of them are generally right."

"They'll come out of there and tear your head off," Lumpkin says, stressing the need to show respect when one is near the hives.

"I would break out in a cold sweat every time I would go out to look at my bees," he recalls.

they can't. Both of them are generally right."

David Stanley and Jim Burton, Joe Neal, Charlie Eldredge and Harrison Locke are the kind of people who think they can. And they're right.

Jerry Lumpkin of Bradford has more than a passing interest in the cucumber fields at Tupelo. If Burton and his associates are successful and their project turns into something really big, Lumpkin's business will prosper. He has been struggling with a market overrun with cheap foreign production. The expansion of vegetable farming in East Arkansas could, using the same basic equipment and livestock, put him into the service sector. It will mean economic survival in a changing world economy.

Lumpkin is the beekeeper who has 300 colonies of bees rented out to Burton, Stanley and Neal to pollinate their cucumber crop. Cucumbers—like other melon-type produce—require insect pollination, and stationing an invasion force of bees in the fields is the only way to get the job done quickly enough. The total population of the 300 hives is about 15 million highly territorial, aggressive, stinger-armed bees.

"They'll come out of there and tear your head off," Lumpkin says, stressing the

need to show respect when one is near the hives.

"Joe Neal was standing by his truck just the other day, and one came and stung him for no reason at all."

Bees do not develop an affection for their keeper, who is forever messing around with their home and stealing their honey. "You'll get stung every day," Lumpkin says, admitting that when he got his first two hives several years ago, he was terrified by these belligerent little bugs.

"I would break out in a cold sweat every time I would go out to look at my bees," he recalls.

He got over his terror enough to take out a big loan from the Small Business Administration and buy 500 hives and go full-time into beekeeping. Today, he has about 1,000 hives, but he figures he needs at least 500 more to pay off his loan and make a decent living. He and his wife and son have struggled for seven years to build the business. They are not discouraged.

Beekeeping is a family affair for the Lumpkins. Jerry and his son Chip, a student at Arkansas State University, take care of the bees. Betty Lumpkin holds down an outside job to keep the family afloat while her husband and son accumulate enough hives to turn a profit.

"I love the honey bees," Lumpkin says. "My son loves them. Really, I think if they didn't make her sick, my wife would love them."

Moving the bees is a sensitive maneuver carried out under cover of darkness.

"I love the honey bees," Lumpkin says. "My son loves them. Really, I think if they didn't make her sick, my wife would love them."

They make Betty Lumpkin deathly ill. And they don't do Chip any good. He's been hospitalized twice with reactions to bee stings and keeps a syringe of epinephrine accessible.

When Jerry was a kid, his father had a hive or two but wouldn't let Jerry so much as look inside. Chip gets to look all he wants.

Renting out large numbers of bees for pollination services is something new for Lumpkin. He provided 12 colonies for an agricultural experiment once, but it was nothing like the Tupelo operation. While he doesn't know if he will make any money placing 300 hives down there, Lumpkin figures that Burton, Stanley and Neal will eventually need a thousand or more hives. That would be profitable.

A disadvantage to service in the cucumber fields is that there are not enough blooms to provide sufficient food for the bees and certainly not enough for the production of surplus honey. The Lumpkins have to compensate by pumping a rich mixture of sugar and water into the hives.

Generally, Lumpkin leaves his hives in the same place all year. Most of them are scattered among soybean fields in Poinsett, Jackson and Independence Counties. Lumpkin has to finagle invitations from farmers. The quid pro quo for hosting a band of the sometimes vicious guests is a slightly improved soybean yield. Not every farmer is willing.

In 1987, the Lumpkins, encouraged by the opportunities at Tupelo, are experimenting with moving the hives around to try for an extra harvest of honey. He planned to move the cucumber pollinators to soybean fields for three or four weeks in August so they could make some honey for him and a supply for themselves before returning to work the fall crop of cucumbers.

Moving the bees is a sensitive maneuver carried out under cover of darkness when the bees are all at home, although, as Lumpkin explains, they may be lying on the outside cooling off from the day's work. They don't like being moved and sometimes register a painful protest.

There is one situation in which the bees tend not to be menacing. That is when they come into Lumpkin's truck to look around, then get disoriented and swarm on the rear window as he drives off.

"They're not mad at you. They forget where they are," Lumpkin says. "You just don't have the heart to turn around and kill them."

One day over at Newport, Jerry and Chip were on their way home to Bradford with bees plastered all over the back window. A couple drove up beside them at a red light, and the woman wanted Jerry's name and address. She said she was writing a book on "strange sights seen in Arkansas" and planned to include him and his bees.

Lumpkin tells the story to illustrate his contention that the general public is more than a little puzzled by beekeepers.

"They think that we're a nutsy breed," he says.

If vegetables go big in the Delta, Lumpkin ought to be recognized as one of a successful breed—the Arkansas entrepreneur.

Heading south from Augusta and Tupelo, the traveler crosses the Grand Prairie region of the Delta, which was an ancient river terrace and is slightly higher than the bottomland, although just as flat. The Grand Prairie is at the heart of Arkansas's rice country, and Arkansas is the leading rice producer in the United States. The Arkansas River flows along the lower edge of the Prairie in its journey to the Mississippi. There is a bridge at Pine

Bluff, a bustling city in a metropolitan area with about 90,000 inhabitants south of the River.

Pine Bluff anchors a narrow, fertile crescent that straddles U.S. Highway 65 from there all the way southeastward to the Louisiana border. Known as Southeast Arkansas, this part of the Delta is separated from northern portion of the Alluvial Plain by the Arkansas River. The dividing line between Southeast Arkansas and the West Gulf Coastal Plain of South Arkansas is the Bayou Bartholomew, a tortuous little stream rising near Pine Bluff and flowing southward to vanish into the lowlands of Louisiana.

As in the rest of the Delta region, agriculture has dominated the economic scene in Southeast Arkansas. New industry was not necessarily welcome in bygone days. With a few exceptions, Delta towns showed little enthusiasm for industrial recruitment, since the farms and existing industries needed most of the available labor.

That has changed. All across the Delta, towns are mobilizing their people and their resources to revive local economies. Responding to the changing nature of agriculture, these communities are actively seeking new business citizens.

Southeast Arkansas is home to two unusual women, both of them civic and polit-

She said she was writing a book on "strange sights seen in Arkansas" and planned to include him and his bees.

ical leaders, who have been calling for years for economic diversification. Their message is having its effect on the entire region.

Rosalie Santini Gould and Charlotte Tillar Schexnayder grew up together in the little town of Tillar just north of McGehee on Highway 65.

Charlotte's father's family helped found the town and gave it the name back in the 1870's. Her mother's people, the Terrys, settled in the Delta in the 1850's.

Rosalie was the daughter of Italian immigrants who had first settled with other Italians in Chicot County, then moved north a few miles to live at Tillar in Desha County.

Rosalie and Charlotte were young at a time when women in the Delta generally were expected to aspire to be good farm wives and mothers.

By the time she was 16 years old, Charlotte was writing for newspapers around Southeast Arkansas. And Rosalie, by age 19, was in medical school at Little Rock.

Charlotte earned a degree at Louisiana State University and came back to become editor of the McGehee Times in 1944. She was one of only two women editors in the state at the time.

She married Melvin Schexnayder, and in 1952

they bought the Dumas Clarion. They've run it ever since. Charlotte is Editor-in-Chief and Publisher. The weekly Clarion is known for its honest and feisty journalism.

Rosalie quit medical school two years into the program and married Joe Gould, a farmer.

Like Charlotte, she had three children.

Until her oldest child was 13 years old, she led a rather conventional life. She was a good farm wife and mother. That year, however, her husband died of a congenital heart defect. She was left with a family to raise and a farm to do it with, if she was of a mind to farm. From then until she retired about ten years ago, she ran the place.

"Not that I'm a feminist or anything," she hastens to explain. "I just feel like if I can do what a man can do, I should have the opportunity."

Today, Rosalie Gould is Mayor of McGehee. In five years on the job, she has earned a reputation for getting things done and she has been educating her constituents to the need for a broader economic base. She speaks candidly about her town's handicaps and strengths and hopefully about its future.

Charlotte Schexnayder is in her second term as a State Representative. She is known as a champion of open

Rosalie and Charlotte were young at a time when women in the Delta generally were expected to aspire to be good farm wives and mothers.

"I just feel like if I can do what a man can do, I should have the opportunity."

33

At Christmas, decorations float in the swamp, sometimes slowing traffic to a crawl on Highway 65, as motorists brake to take a look. A lighted nativity scene graces the still waters.

One year, a duck laid eggs in the manger.

government, better education, diversified agriculture and economic development.

These women are part of the hope of the Delta.

Mayor Gould's rise to political prominence in McGehee came after she quit farming when her children were all grown. A devout Catholic, she has deep-seated convictions about an individual's obligations to society.

"To be productive," she contends, "you've got to push yourself. Most of us are lazy."

(It should be noted here that besides being a full-time Mayor, she is a member of the boards of 14 nonprofit organizations.)

Her first public position in McGehee was on the Parks Commission, where she was instrumental in launching an effort to convert a dense swamp at the edge of town into a park.

In 1976 she was elected to the City Council, but she resigned a couple of years later. The Mayor at that time got angry with her because she wouldn't back his plan to raise privilege taxes. He shouted. She shouted back. Ms. Gould resigned, feeling that public officials ought to be able to handle their differences better than that.

In 1982, people started urging her to run for Mayor. She entered the race and won without a runoff over three male opponents.

McGehee is looking better these days. The swamp is now an unusual and appealing park. Across the road from it are the swimming pool and several ballfields that are the envy of the region. They play a lot of ball in McGehee.

At Christmas, decorations float in the swamp, sometimes slowing traffic to a crawl on Highway 65, as motorists brake to take a look. A lighted nativity scene graces the still waters.

One year, a duck laid eggs in the manger.

Downtown, you'll find flowers along the streets and a smaller park. Out east of town, an eighty-acre tract awaits industrial development. The city bought the land at the Mayor's suggestion—or insistence.

McGehee hasn't had much experience at trying to bring businesses into town. For years, the strong agricultural base of the area and the Missouri-Pacific Railroad shops and switching yards lulled the town into a deadly complacency. Mayor Gould said that back when Potlatch first wanted to build a plant east of town on the Mississippi River, local officials showed no interest at all. Potlatch built in spite of the cool reception.

Now that agriculture is in decline and the new owners of the railroad are slowly

"We're going to bring industry in here," the Mayor says confidently. "There's no two ways about it."

"There is no way that I could have survived for more than 30 years with this newspaper without a vision of what this newspaper and this area could become."

closing down the shops, McGehee is mighty proud to have Potlatch towering over the Father of Waters.

"We're going to bring industry in here," the Mayor says confidently. "There's no two ways about it."

Dumas has probably shown more foresight over the years than any other town in Southeast Arkansas. Rosalie Gould says admiringly that Dumas has been recruiting for at least 25 years. Just a couple of years ago, the town adopted a 20-year industrial development program. When Sunbeam announced that it was abandoning its Dumas operations after 20 years, the shakers and movers of Dumas got the names of 250 industries, divided them up and started calling. They brought in the Hussman Company to take over the empty Sunbeam plant.

Through her weekly editorials and in feature articles and anywhere else she can get an audience, Charlotte Schexnayder has been preaching economic diversity for years. In the summer of 1987, farmers who are making tentative moves away from the traditional row crops of the Delta found themselves in a series of Clarion feature articles.

She and Rosalie Gould are leaders in a coalition of individuals up and down Highway 65 from Grady to

Eudora working on projects that will benefit the whole region. Right now, they're after a new bridge across the river into Bolivar County, Mississippi. And they want Highway 65 widened to four lanes.

Running for the General Assembly just seemed like a natural progression to Charlotte. She was raised in a family that liked politics and talked politics. She has studied government, reported on government, chided and goaded it. When she asked Melvin what he thought about her going into politics, he didn't hesitate a minute.

"You've been wanting to run for 20 years," he said. "Go on and do it."

To those who suggest that it might be a conflict of interest for a newspaper-woman to sit in the Legislature, Charlotte replies:

"It's no more of a conflict to have a communicator than a lawyer."

Anyway, she argues, the Assembly needs a cross-section of the people.

In the Arkansas General Assembly, just as she does back home, Ms. Schexnayder preaches foresight and planning, two of the hallmarks of her way of doing business.

"There is no way that I could have survived for more than 30 years with this newspaper without a vision of

She cried when he moved her to Calico Rock 14 years ago so he could take his first and only assignment as a trooper. She wouldn't leave now.

Moad is a no-nonsense kind of fellow. He went up to City Hall and got the Aldermen not only to authorize an Industrial Development Committee but also—and this was shrewd—to let him select the members.

what this newspaper and this area could become."

Talking to Charlotte Schexnayder and Rosalie Gould and seeing what is already taking place in Southeast Arkansas, you cannot help but believe that in a just a few more years, much of that vision will be reality.

Not all the leaders of community efforts around Arkansas come from the ranks of public officials or even from the usual cadre of business types. A little town far up in North Arkansas is the most surprising in this regard.

The town is Calico Rock, a quiet place perched on calico-colored bluffs overlooking the White River. Although the town is just about 350 feet above sea level, the countryside, in the eastern foothills of the Ozarks, is fairly rugged, lightly populated and heavily forested.

A businessman speeding along state Highway 5 around Calico Rock stands a chance of getting a ticket from State Trooper Del Moad. And, after he writes the ticket, Moad is likely to ask the offender to move his business to Calico Rock.

If the businessman is interested, Moad will show him the Calico Rock Industrial Park and loose a battery of trained volunteers on him who will extol the virtues of living and working in this town of 1,200 inhabitants.

Moad is more than a trooper. He sells a little real estate and, every spring, does income tax work. His wife Liz operates the White River Insurance Agency, a business they started several years ago. He's an Arkansas boy, born and reared at Rogers. Liz is a California girl who married Del when he was a Los Angeles policeman. She cried when he moved her to Calico Rock 14 years ago so he could take his first and only assignment as a trooper. She wouldn't leave now. It's home for the Moads and their two children.

Two years ago, Moad finally got all he could take of gloomy coffee talk, people sitting around moaning about how Calico Rock was going to die. But nobody was doing anything to prevent the presumed inevitable demise of the quaint little town on the calico bluffs.

Moad is a no-nonsense kind of fellow. He went up to City Hall and got the Aldermen not only to authorize an Industrial Development Committee but also—and this was shrewd—to let him select the members. Meaning to get something done, he enlisted a group of people he knew would work.

They called in field workers from the Arkansas Industrial Development Commission and got themselves trained in prospecting for economic development.

Then, just as the Committee was poised to have its first town meeting to whip up community support, two companies already doing business there announced they were pulling out.

Arkansas Kraft of Morrilton said it would be closing its buy yard, thus throwing about 100 independent cutters out of work. While the town was reeling from that shattering announcement, one of Calico Rock's native sons and best success stories, David McNeil, announced that he was taking McNeil Trucking Company to Little Rock.

McNeil employed about 120 people, some of them drivers who lived elsewhere but most of them local folks. Born and reared at Calico Rock, McNeil taught school for a while after graduation from college, then started his trucking company in 1964.

By the time of the town meeting in December 1985, the Industrial Development Committee and its mission had taken on a sense of urgency. Two hundred people showed up, about one-sixth of the population. The Committee and an AIDC representative told them the town needed to reactivate its defunct Industrial Development Corporation, buy a tract of land for an industrial park and get Calico Rock in good shape to show off to anybody who would give it an audience.

A week later, at least 150 residents were back to meet again, many of them with their checkbooks. This time they bought shares in the Industrial Development Corporation and elected its Board of Directors and officers. Not surprisingly, Del Moad was elected President.

Moad's approach was to involve as many people as possible in the effort. One of the first committees he appointed was the one to locate a site for the industrial park, which needed to be a fairly level piece of ground as close in as possible. The committee settled on a 30-acre tract adjoining the City Park, but the banker who owned it really didn't want to sell.

"We told him, 'you're not going to have a bank if we don't have a town,' " Moad said.

So effective were they at convincing the man to sell that he offered it at a bargain price—$45,000 for 30 fairly level acres in the city limits of a hilly town, with city water running right to the edge of the site.

In just 181 days, the Board members raised the money to pay for the land.

In the meantime, David McNeil was studying the changes he was seeing in the community's attitude. He had felt more than a little taken for granted. He had even figured that the town really didn't care whether he

"We told him, 'you're not going to have a bank if we don't have a town,' " Moad said.

In just 181 days, the Board members raised the money to pay for the land.

was there or not. From an economic standpoint, it would make sense for him to move closer to the major truck routes. When he saw the town get behind the Industrial Development Corporation, he began to reconsider.

About the same time, the Corporation Board of Directors, seeking ways to help existing businesses, got the town declared an "enterprise zone," which offers considerable state tax breaks to participating companies. The Board of Directors also got the town enrolled in a federally-funded program which offers salary subsidies to companies providing training to the unemployed.

McNeil changed his mind and announced he would stay in Calico Rock. Subsequently, he spent a million dollars expanding his fleet, offices and terminal. Today, he runs nearly 100 trucks with a staff of about 170 people. "I'm here to stay," he says. "I can't leave now." Reed Perryman, a former Alderman, became mayor in 1987, about the time he was elected President of the Arkansas Pharmacists Association. He's excited: "We're just right on the verge of something really good."

Perryman, who served as a School Board member for ten years, sees the 500-student Calico Rock School District as one of the town's selling points. To assure that it would meet the tough new state school standards, the town voted by two-to-one to more than double the millage rate—from 19 to 39 mills.

At mid-summer in 1987, the Industrial Development Corporation was in serious negotiations with two companies.

"We're that close on them," Moad, holding up the tip of a finger, said of a corporation that would open a new plant with 40 employees and plans for an eventual work force of 200.

The other prospect would employ about 20 workers in the production of cedar chests.

While Moad and Perryman and their colleagues on the Board have learned how to promote their town, they aren't relying on good salesmanship to compensate for inadequacies. If they need something, they go to work to get it.

In the future, Calico Rock will need a bigger sewer system. The possibility of a joint effort with Pineville, a smaller town nearby, is already being explored.

Also, Calico Rock has no airport, an amenity some industries consider indispensable.

"We're working on that," Moad said.

If the recent history of Calico Rock is a reliable

"We're just right on the verge of something really good."

The remotest, hardest-to-find woodworking shop in all of Arkansas is in the valley of the Big Piney Creek, one of the loveliest, purest streams in the state.

As the poet says, "the woods are lovely, dark and deep." Furthermore, the road out of Nail is narrow, rough and steep.

guide, the town will get a new sewer system and an airport and whatever else it needs to assure its citizens of future livelihood.

Traveling westward from Calico Rock takes you deeper and higher into the embrace of the Ozark Mountains. One of the discoveries awaiting the curious visitor to this pristine region is that many have settled here deliberately seeking a respite from the pressures of urban living. Many natives, aware of what a treasure this environment is, have simply never left. Making a living in the mountains hasn't always been easy, but a lot of imaginative and creative people have managed to live quite comfortably and simply in the quiet grandeur of North Arkansas.

Here is the story of a group of enterprising craftsmen who have combined the rustic life of an isolated Ozarks valley with a growing business whose products end up in some of the finest homes and offices in the state:

The remotest, hardest-to-find woodworking shop in all of Arkansas is in the valley of the Big Piney Creek, one of the loveliest, purest streams in the state.

If you want to visit, call first and find out how to get there. If you go by the mailing address, you'll end up at

Ozone, 40 miles south of the Walnut Fork Woodshop. The telephone comes out of Nail, and the shop is just six miles south of that out-of-the-way community. But six miles south of Nail is not an ordinary six miles. At an elevation of about 2,200 feet, Nail is at one of the highest points in the Ozarks. The woodshop is more than a thousand feet down the side of the mountain.

As the poet says, "the woods are lovely, dark and deep." Furthermore, the road out of Nail is narrow, rough and steep.

They're nice folks down at the woodshop, though. If you care enough to drop in on them once, they'll show you the back way out.

What you find on the valley floor is a small colony of true craftsmen using the most modern equipment to perform some of the oldest techniques of wood fabrication. They work mostly in oak, cherry and walnut, woods native to the Ozarks. Much of it comes in fresh-cut and must be air-dried for several months before they move it into their solar kiln to cure for about six weeks.

The handiwork of the Walnut Fork craftsmen adorns a number of fine houses around the state. If you should get into the Governor's Mansion and find yourself admiring the new circular stairway

If you should get into the Governor's Mansion and find yourself admiring the new circular stairway of oak and walnut, you would be looking at the work of the boys at Walnut Fork.

of oak and walnut, you would be looking at the work of the boys at Walnut Fork. It's probably safe to assume that they're prouder of the Mansion staircase than of anything else they have made.

The woodshop was built in the summer of 1980, one of the hottest and driest in Arkansas history. The shop is done in "timberframing," a technique popular in New England two centuries ago. Heavy, rough-cut timbers held together by intricate pinned joints (with no bolts or nails) form the superstructure in a timberframed building. The craftsmen leave these timbers exposed, lending an appearance of strength and antiquity.

Walnut Fork was raised on Labor Day weekend in 1980 by about 50 friends. The timbers had been painstakingly cut and notched in a woodshop at Flippin, then trucked into the valley. The crowd lifted them into place and pinned the intricate joints in a weekend of work and fun.

The woodshop is the brainchild of Dr. Bob Ahrens, his boyhood friend John Alexander and Vincent Leyendecker. Alexander and Leyendecker run the shop with from four to six other craftsmen. Ahrens, a physician at Yellville 90 miles to the northeast, has a cabin nearby and spends his leisure time working in the shop.

Alexander, the first to settle in the valley, has a degree in physics from the University of Arkansas at Fayetteville. At one time, he contemplated a career in the space program, but he got his credentials about the time the space program was winding down in the faint afterglow of the lunar landing. Woodworking had been a hobby of his since childhood in Mountain Home, where he and Ahrens grew up. So he turned to building houses, but that business fell on hard times in the late 1970's, a victim of mortgage rates that ran into the teens.

Alexander and Leyendecker started working with Ahrens in the shop he had at his home in Flippin, doing cabinet and furniture work, and they conceived the idea of Walnut Fork.

Though they have chosen to live and work at considerable distance from the rush of modern life, the sale of their products depends on people who have done well in the mainstream. What they turn out at Walnut Fork is a far cry from the polyurethaned pine bread boxes, potato bins and napkin holders you might associate with country woodworking. They do custom cabinets, doors, window frames, stairs and furniture, built to last for generations. And it is expensive, the kind of heirloom-quality work sought by architects and interior designers.

Alexander found two log cabins—one oak, the other pine—in the surrounding hills and took them apart, carefully numbering each log.

The first sounds likely to greet a visitor to Walnut Fork are the notes of a Beethoven symphony or a work of Mozart or some other great classical piece.

Besides Alexander, Leyendecker and two other craftsmen at the shop live with their families in the valley. From a practical standpoint, it makes sense to live close by because of the difficulty of getting in and out of the valley. If you spend some time there and visit their homes, you realize that it is for more than the sake of convenience that they have chosen such splendid isolation.

Alexander found two log cabins—one oak, the other pine—in the surrounding hills and took them apart, carefully numbering each log. Then he reassembled them at opposite ends of a rock foundation he built on a hillside overlooking the valley. He joined the two with a kitchen in the middle and used timberframing to provide a half-story overhead. He put a wide porch around three sides.

The other homes in the valley are at various stages of construction. All are done in the classic style of timberframing.

What you find in the valley is a harmonious blend of modernity and antiquity. Some of the houses still have no electricity and no running water. The shop has some state-of-the-art electrical equipment—a 38-inch belt sander, for example, and power tools to do mortice-and-tenon joints. There is no air-conditioning, but there is a thoroughly modern sprinkler system to protect against fire. You don't hear many of the noises of civilization down in the valley, except for the saws, drills and planers.

The first sounds likely to greet a visitor to Walnut Fork are the notes of a Beethoven symphony or a work of Mozart or some other great classical piece. Bob Ahrens likes to bathe in primitive style in Walnut Creek just above its confluence with the Big Piney, but he likes his classical music on a respectable set of speakers.

From the solitude of the Big Piney Valley to the thriving area around Fayetteville in Northwest Arkansas is scarcely more than a hour's drive. Fayetteville is the home of the original and main campus of the University of Arkansas, with an enrollment of 13,688 in the fall of 1987. The Fayetteville-Springdale-Rogers-Bentonville strip along U.S. Highway 71 is in the midst of an economic boom. With the University, the poultry industry, trucking companies, the headquarters of one of the country's largest discount chains and many other industries, the area enjoys the lowest unemployment rate in the state.

With the quiet rural areas close by, beautiful

"The fellow that was Mayor wasn't feeling good, and he asked me to take his place," Carter says. "I thought it was for three months. Turned out it was for three years and three months.

The ways of government are still a little puzzling to the Mayor, who has owned a business for 15 years and doesn't have much patience with waste or bureaucratic red tape.

Beaver Lake and several smaller bedroom communities clustered around the larger towns, this section of the state offers easy access to a wide variety of living environments.

Within ten years, Highway 71 will be four-lane all the way up from Interstate 40 just east of Fort Smith. The economic implications of that project are enormous, and some of those bedroom towns plan to take full advantage of them. One of those towns is West Fork, just south of Fayetteville.

Bill Carter is Mayor of West Fork. He really didn't ask for the job. But now that he's got it, he figures he'll stay around for awhile.

"The fellow that was Mayor wasn't feeling good, and he asked me to take his place," Carter says. "I thought it was for three months. Turned out if was for three years and three months."

Then he stood for election in 1986 with no opposition.

"I kinda enjoy it," he says.

West Fork has about 1,500 residents and lies west of U.S. Highway 71 five miles south of Fayetteville. It gets a little bigger just about every time the City Council meets. Word is out that it pays to be a part of West Fork. So adjoining landowners keep asking to be annexed.

"We're selling them on it," says the Mayor.

What he's selling is basic city services and the notion that there is a bright future for West Fork. Since Carter took office in 1983, city government has been lively and aggressive. There's a new City Hall, animal control, an expanded library, a lot more pavement, a reorganized administration, a growing City Park and plans for a Community Center and an Industrial Park.

"If it gets dull, we start another project," Carter says.

The ways of government are still a little puzzling to the Mayor, who has owned a business for 15 years and doesn't have much patience with waste or bureaucratic red tape. After four years in office, he has managed to get control of things at the West Fork City Hall. As for government bureaucracy beyond the city limits, he says:

"There's nothing you're going to do about it. I found that out."

Carter is not one to whine, though. He believes that if there is a way to do something without involving the federal or state governments, the city ought to bear its own load. Take the new Municipal Building, for instance.

The old City Hall was too small. Right next door

He came up with a plan for buying the old store and remodeling it and doing it all a lot cheaper, without any outside help.

"I drew it first on a napkin," he says, "down at the coffee shop."

was a vacant brick building that went up in 1926 and had been used for a lot of different purposes. When Carter was a kid, his father ran a grocery store there, and Carter delivered for him.

The city approved a bond issue for a new building, and the Council had intended to seek some state or federal funds to help. But, Carter says, "we found out it was going to take three years."

He came up with a plan for buying the old store and remodeling it and doing it all a lot cheaper, without any outside help.

"I drew it first on a napkin," he says, "down at the coffee shop."

Then a staff member at the North Arkansas Planning and Development District transferred the plan to blueprints. That saved an architect's fee. Carter and Butch Bartholomew, the city Business Manager, took the place of a general contractor and called for bids on the various components of the building. They did a little ground work on the bidding by talking with potential suppliers to let them know money was tight and how nice it would be if they bid a bargain price.

For less than $125,000, they ended up with a handsome 5,000-square-foot building with city offices, the

Police Department, the Municipal Courtroom and a community room with a kitchenette. That price also included remodeling the old City Hall and dedicating the space to the Library.

Carter may be new to politics, but he seems to have the right instincts. When it came time to choose a color for the outside, he and Bartholomew painted swatches on the side of the building and left chalk for townsfolk to indicate their preference. As luck would have it, the people chose what Carter thought they should—beige.

One thing that bothered Carter right off after he took office was the time-honored practice of closing City Hall during the noon hour. "Heavens," he says, "we're here to serve the public, not us."

You can call or come by at noon nowadays.

Since he is what he terms a "free-gratis Mayor," Carter figured he needed someone in charge during the day. The city now has about 10 employees. So he got the City Council to make Bartholomew the Business Manager with full authority in the Mayor's absence.

Bartholomew, like Carter, is a West Fork native. He started working for the city in 1971 while he was still a student at the University of Arkansas. He was Superintendent of City Utilities. Even

Carter, who says women "get out and get moving," has developed a number of committees for the various projects and has made sure he has a lot of women involved.

though he has a new title now, he still sees to the operation of the water and sewer systems.

Water comes from the White River behind a dam in the middle of town.

Carter operates on the belief that his people expect the city to run a tight ship, enforcing the laws and making the place as liveable as possible. He also figures this is the best way to attract the kind of new business and industry West Fork is seeking.

State law allows a city zoning authority up to five miles outside its borders. West Fork became the first of the little towns in the area to begin exercising this authority. Now several are doing so.

When the town celebrated its centennial in 1985 with three days of merriment, residents really cleaned up the place. The Mayor says that started an awareness of the town's appearance that has persisted since then.

West Fork was in the middle of developing a City Park when the state and federal funds dried up. Now he is determined that, one way or another, the Park will be finished.

West Fork has a lot of teenagers, who find little to their leisure-time liking in town. Carter says they generally end up taking off to

Fayetteville. The city now is about to deal with that by erecting a Community Center where its youth can go and eat out of snack machines, have music and dance. Carter hopes to open it about three nights a week with adult volunteers to provide supervision.

West Fork has had a ball program for years. By next year, the Mayor wants to have the Park fully opened so that the city can also offer something for kids who don't play ball.

Traditionally, city government in West Fork was the province of men. In the last five years, however, the town has elected two women to the City Council. Carter, who says women "get out and get moving," has developed a number of committees for the various projects and has made sure he has a lot of women involved.

Behind all this activity is a sort of broad timetable in Carter's mind. Presently, West Fork has no businesses beyond a few retail establishments. Carter sees that changing in the next decade if the town is prepared.

Within ten years, the four-lane highway will come from I-40 up along the present western boundary of West Fork and on to Missouri. Carter is unperturbed by the fact that the freeway will take his house and swim-

"We'll be booming in the next ten years," Carter says.

Will he stay around to see that happen?

"As long as people cooperate and want to grow," he says. "If they don't want to grow, I don't want any part of it."

ming pool. He and his wife will move into the heart of town.

He sees the new highway as an opportunity for West Fork to attract some light industry and grow.

"We'll be booming in the next ten years," Carter says.

Will he stay around to see that happen?

"As long as people cooperate and want to grow," he says. "If they don't want to grow, I don't want any part of it."

Carter reckons the voters gave him their answer when they re-elected him in 1986.

Highway 71 from West Fork to Interstate 40 at Alma takes you over some of the highest points in the Ozarks and past many of the broadest, most scenic vistas. From Alma, it is just a short drive of about 15 miles to Fort Smith, a highly industrialized city at the heart of a rapidly growing metropolitan area of about 180,000 inhabitants. Situated on the Arkansas River, Fort Smith has been involved in carefully planned economic development for at least three decades. Today, a well-paid work force turns out a wide range of goods from appliances and furniture to molded plastics, peanut products, electric motors and fine liqueurs.

Observers of the industrial scene in Arkansas say Fort Smith has benefitted from longevity, persistence and energy in its business leaders. One man often mentioned is the late Paul Latture, whose long tenure as Director of the Fort Smith Chamber of Commerce is regarded as a major factor in the continuity and success of the city's development program.

The city also has a rich history dating from 1817, two years before Arkansas became a territory. It is probably best known historically as the home of Judge Isaac C. Parker, the famous "Hanging Judge." Parker meted out a tough and often fatal style of justice as Federal Judge over the Indian Territory (now Oklahoma) from 1875 to 1896. His courtroom and other relics of the period still draw many visitors from Arkansas and elsewhere.

These little vignettes are offered as a sampler of Arkansas people, Arkansas places and the Arkansas spirit. The pages available here would allow no more than a brief look inside the lives of a few communities and people. Those mentioned here are no more or no less important than any other locale or Arkansas citizens.

Arkansas is proud of its heritage and past accomplishments and eagerly looks to the future with great

Outside, the graduates were restless. Some slipped into their robes 45 minutes early. Gaylynne Vaughan did. She was the salutatorian and had a speech to make. Another girl was near tears. She told a boy she was not ready to graduate. But she had her gown on early.

At 8 o'clock sharp, the crowd hushed to hear the first strains of "Pomp and Circumstance." Eyes watered.

anticipation. But Arkansans may be proudest of their children to whom the future will belong. Hence, this essay closes with the account of a high school graduation which was not unlike hundreds of other high school graduations that go on every year in Arkansas.

It happens every May —a preview of summer, a day or so when heat and humidity are about the same. That's how it was on May 21, 1987, when 33 graduating seniors at the West Side High School at Greers Ferry donned their mortarboards and made their parents proud.

Inside, the gymnasium was heating up early. Fans drew fresh air across the end walls. In the middle, where aunts and uncles, mothers and daddies and faithful friends would sit, the sultry air did not stir at all.

Outside, the graduates were restless. Some slipped into their robes 45 minutes early. Gaylynne Vaughan did. She was the salutatorian and had a speech to make. Another girl was near tears. She told a boy she was not ready to graduate. But she had her gown on early.

The crowd started arriving well ahead of time. By 8 p.m. the good seats were gone. In a little community like this, the school commands a wide loyalty. On Sundays, the people go off to their separate churches. But for football and basketball, open house and graduation, they will flock to the school. More than 500 came to see those 33 kids graduate.

J.B. Hunt, the trucking magnate, got there a little early with the notes for his speech on a three-by-five index card in his shirt pocket. He wore his gold dollar-sign cufflinks. J.B. grew up around Greers Ferry but never got this far in school. He was proud to be the graduation speaker. Outside, old friends and kinfolks showed they were proud that he was one of their own who had done well. A woman walked up behind him and announced, "I got to hug this millionaire." J.B. knew her by name.

At 8 o'clock sharp, the crowd hushed to hear the first strains of "Pomp and Circumstance." Eyes watered. Letha Chadwell beamed. These seniors came out of her second kindergarten class 13 years ago.

As the music faded, the Reverend Rick Domerese of the Lone Star Baptist Church delivered an invocation that was heartfelt and practical.

"Father," he said, "we pray that you will just bless them and open the doors of employment to them."

Then Gaylynne Vaughan had her moment of glory. She was bold and optimistic. "We control our destinies," she declared, proclaiming the Class of 1987 "a class that is ready to take on life and all it has to offer." Gaylynne earned two scholarships.

Scott Vaughan was the valedictorian. He bid his classmates "a formal farewell" and later formally received a four-year, $4,200 scholarship.

All told, the Class of 1987 received more than $30,000 in scholarships. Twenty-four of them plan to continue their education. Eleven were honor graduates.

J.B. Hunt was introduced as a man who got his start selling wood chips for chicken litter. Today he heads a trucking company operating all over the continental United States.

He told the graduates they had taken the first step to becoming rich, but he warned them that wealth would not mean much if they forgot other things—"like the Lord Jesus Christ," he said.

He admonished them to work hard and fast.

"Don't wait around for your grandfather to die and leave you a few bucks," he said. "Nobody's going to give you anything."

J.B. took some time to talk directly to the boys.

"I teach a class to my truck drivers on how to get

along with your wife," he said, going on to offer them a few jewels from the curriculum.

"Unless you find someone you can't live without," he said, "don't marry her."

He told them to plan on marrying only one woman and staying with her the rest of their lives.

"And tell your wife you love her," he said. "I tell Johnelle I love her twice every day."

Johnelle was in the audience. She nodded approvingly.

After the graduates received their diplomas from Walter Murphree, president of the West Side School Board, the ceremony was about over.

Rick Domerese stood again to call down a heavenly benediction. A baby cried, reminding the people of Greers Ferry that there would be other hot May nights like this.

"Don't wait around for your grandfather to die and leave you a few bucks," he said. "Nobody's going to give you anything."

"And tell your wife you love her," he said. "I tell Johnelle I love her twice every day."

Johnelle was in the audience. She nodded approval.

47

You have read about the diversity of the Arkansas people and geography. Now, in the following pages, you will see in full color a sampling of the many faces of the Arkansas landscape.

The countryside, the little towns and the cities are, like the people, diverse. Lifestyle, which is closely tied to the style of the land, varies from one region to another, giving rise to a diversity of cultures. The way the ages have sculpted the terrain and the boundaries Arkansas's forefathers chose for the state combine to make this rich variety of geography and people easily accessible. If you tire of the world around you and long for a change in the lay of the land, an entirely different view is never far away. Some of the transitions are sudden and dramatic, particularly between the Delta and the uplands.

The Little Rock metropolitan area is peculiarly well situated to take advantage of this smorgasbord of terrains. From downtown Little Rock, situated on a prominence safely elevated above the Arkansas River, you can go west into the foothills of the Ouachita Mountains. Just to the north across the river lie the last of the Ouachita foothills. Within an hour's travel time going northward, you will traverse the Arkansas River Valley and reach the foothills of the Ozark Mountains. Just beyond the eastern edge of town is the most western reach of the Delta. To the south is the region geologists call the Gulf Coastal Plain, rolling country, home of Arkansas's immense forest industry.

The photographs in this section are presented with quotations from more than a score of national publications whose writers have commented on Arkansas. Their observations showed great perception, and their permission to reprint them here is acknowledged and appreciated.

This collection was first printed as a separate book in 1986 as part of the Sesquicentennial Celebration.

The original publication was made possible through the cooperative efforts of the Office of the Governor, the Arkansas Game and Fish Commission, the Arkansas Highway and Transportation Department, the Department of Arkansas Heritage, the Arkansas Industrial Development Commission, the Arkansas Department of Parks and Tourism and the Sesquicentennial Sponsors.

The production of this color section was a joint effort of the Woods Brothers Agency and Cranford Johnson Robinson Associates, both prominent advertising agencies based in Little Rock. For the color photography, we are indebted to some of the state's most outstanding photographers: Ron Finley, A.C. Haralson, Bernie Jungkind, Joe Rice, Hubert Smith and Edgar Cheatham.

Arkansas according to others.

You have read an insider's view of the state. Now we offer the comments of journalists from all over the country who have come to judge us for themselves.

Clearly, the beauty of Arkansas lingered in their memories when they got back home and began to write about what they had discovered within our borders.

Their words will tell you a lot about Arkansas.

ake pleasure in our differenc

There is no one perfect example f Arkansas. Nothing in the world an be singled out to say, "This is hat Arkansas is." We like it iat way.

Our geography is too diverse to e described one way or another. ach part of the state has its own nique heritage which, in turn, has volved its own life style. And just s the land and the people vary, so o the things we produce. What ou see in Arkansas depends on here you look.

If you are looking for a place to lay, this is the land for it. If you

e looking to build and grow, rkansas has the resources. And ich part of Arkansas has different ferings for work or play. What ou find in Arkansas is determined y what you seek.

The best way to appreciate rkansas is to take it as it is. onsider all of the parts and take easure in the differences. Travel ew roads to new adventures and llow old trails to the state's eginnings. Take to the woods and aters to share in nature's bounty. isit the cities, towns and villages. earn the different personalities.

You can find life pretty much any ay you want it in Arkansas. Just emember — some of us hear a olin while others hear a fiddle. nd we like it that way.

A unique tapestry of mountains, plains, and fertile delta, Arkansas' heritage..."
TRAVEL SOUTH

The broad White River is world famous for its productive float fishing . . ."
FIELD AND STREAM

The 94-mile stretch of river . . . may well be bass fishing's best-kept secret."
BASSMASTER

njoy freshwater fishing that is the equal of any in the United States."

ESQUIRE

I t's all here: water, mountains, big-city excitement and many of our nation's most refreshing spas. Arkansas even has its own wines." SATURDAY EVENING POST "outhern hospitality and business savvy combine to make Arkansas a state visitors call delightful and the down-to-earth call home."

CORPORATE MEETINGS & INCENTIVES

No matter where you're going . . . your initial route out of town should be an easy one."

DESTINATIONS

Ballet Arkansas has brought magnificent programs . . . Mikhail Baryshnikov was just 'one of the company' . . ."

SKY

The best of the University Museum's . . . treasures is 'Big Boy,' a bauxite effigy pipe that is widely recognized as one of the most important examples of prehistoric culture in North America." THE EXPLORER

A
rkansas Symphony Orchestra has attracted outstanding conductors and professional instrumentalists."

SKY

T
he Saunders Memorial Museum . . . one of the finest collections of antique handguns in the entire country."

HOBBIES

The Arkansas Repertory Theatre ... everything from original plays to Shakespeare, *Dracula,* and *Waiting for Lefty.*" TOWN AND COUNTRY

A gently rolling countryside of fields and woods and brushy creeks."

What draws people to these hills is their wild beauty."

U.S. NEWS AND WORLD REPORT

The Thorncrown Chapel is the most striking example of what might be called the 'New Age of Metaphysical Architecture' in this country."

NEWSWEEK

"The Mid-America Center . . .
The building's lively forms
arouse continuing interest, and
its displays are expected to attract
about a million visitors this year."

ARCHITECTURAL RECORD

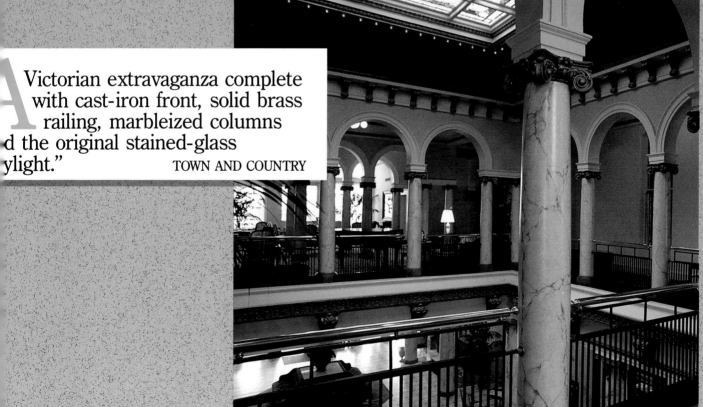

"A Victorian extravaganza complete
with cast-iron front, solid brass
railing, marbleized columns
and the original stained-glass
skylight."

TOWN AND COUNTRY

"The huge rice-growing, green timber area attracts more ducks, and particularly mallards, than any place on the Mississippi Flyway, providing a duck hunting bonanza of magnificent quality and tremendous proportions."

NORTH AMERICAN HUNTER

F

ew states celebrate fall with the verve of Arkansas . . . peppered with festivals."

ENDLESS VACATION

The Ozark Folk Center at
Mountain View has become one
of the nation's primary showcases
for artisans and musicians . . ."

DALLAS MORNING NEWS

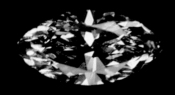

One of the few places in
the world where people
can go into the fields
and prospect for their own
raw diamonds."

REDBOOK

O aklawn, one of the top tracks between New York and California."
TOWN AND COUNTRY

"A genuine statewide spirit of excellence in athletics."

COLORADO SPRINGS
GAZETTE TELEGRAPH

H uge blue lakes . . . quiet glades by clear pools . . ." WASHINGTON POST

W hether you are an Olympic paddler, a white water buff, an artist, a photographer, a family in search of experience, or just doing what you love best, Arkansas' rivers set a standard of excellence." CANOE

I f the American Dream won't work here, it won't work anywhere."   EBONY

The quotations on the preceding pages were only the highlights of what these visitors had to say. Below, we present the larger context from which these words of praise were drawn.

SPREAD TWO

Travel South magazine – Winter/Spring 1984-85
"A unique tapestry of mountains, plains, and fertile delta, Arkansas' heritage is part Western frontier and part Old South. Throughout, there's a true small-town friendliness ready to welcome you whether you opt for taking it easy or rising to the challenge of the out-of-doors. Choose contemporary cityscapes or country recreation that takes full advantage of The Natural State's resources: 9,700 miles of streams and rivers, 600,000 acres of lakes, hot springs, vast forestlands and mountains, and even a diamond field where you can keep what you find."

SPREAD THREE

Gerald Almy, *Field & Stream* magazine – April 1983
"The broad White River is world famous for its productive float fishing, and the North Fork, a tributary of the White, is considered one of the most fertile trout streams in the nation."

Bassmaster magazine – July/August 1984
"The 94-mile stretch of river near Pine Bluff, Ark., may well be bass fishing's best-kept secret."

Gene Lyons, *Esquire* magazine – January 1983
"I love Little Rock because I can put a flatboat into the Arkansas River inside the city limits and enjoy freshwater fishing that is the equal of any in the United States, or into any of a dozen beautiful, forest-ringed lakes within an hour's drive."

SPREAD FOUR

Maynard Good Stoddard, *Saturday Evening Post* magazine – August 1985
"It's all here: water, mountains, big-city excitement and many of our nation's most refreshing spas. Arkansas even has its own wines."

Corporate Meetings & Incentives magazine – August 1985
"Southern hospitality and business savvy combine to make Arkansas a state visitors call delightful and the down-to-earth call home."

SPREAD FIVE

Destinations, published by American Bus Association, November 1985
"No matter where you're going – the beauty of the Arkansas Ozarks in Eureka Springs, the soothing nature of Hot Springs, the music center of Pine Bluff, the diamond fields near Murfreesboro – your initial route out of town should be an easy one. The major roads of Arkansas all run into Little Rock like spokes on a wheel."

SPREAD SIX

Connoisseur magazine – August 1984
"The collection's inaugural exhibition (which runs through September) contains some of the best American drawings I have seen anywhere in this country." (In reference to the Arkansas Arts Center at Little Rock.)

Edgar and Patricia Cheatham, *Sky* magazine, March 1985. This has been reprinted through the courtesy of Halsey Publishing Co., publishers of *Sky* magazine.
"A mere six years in existence, Ballet Arkansas has brought magnificent programs to Little Rock – the Louisville Ballet, in which Mikhail Baryshnikov was just 'one of the company'; Dance Theatre of Harlem, with its rave-review version of *Giselle* in a Creole setting; and the Houston Ballet's stunning *Sleeping Beauty*."

The Explorer Magazine, Cleveland Museum of Natural History – Fall 1985
"Regarded as the best of the University Museum's nine treasures is 'Big Boy,' a bauxite effigy pipe that is widely recognized as one of the most important examples of prehistoric culture in North America."

SPREAD SEVEN

Edgar and Patricia Cheatham, *Sky* magazine, March 1985. This has been reprinted through the courtesy of Halsey Publishing Co., publishers of *Sky* magazine.
"Since 1966, the Little Rock-based Arkansas Symphony Orchestra has attracted outstanding conductors and professional instrumentalists."

Hobbies magazine – October 1981
"The recreational opportunities offered by the Ozarks region draw thousands of vacationers to the area each year. Many of these pause in Berryville to visit the Saunders Memorial Museum, opened to the public in 1956. Housed in the red brick building trimmed with Ozark marble is the collection of Col. C. Burton "Buck" Saunders, which contains silver, furniture, glassware, fabrics, and Indian artifacts – plus one of the finest collections of antique handguns in the entire country."

Town & Country magazine – May 1981
"The Arkansas Repertory Theatre brings adventurous professional theatre to Little Rock, everything from original plays to Shakespeare, *Dracula* and *Waiting for Lefty*."

SPREAD EIGHT

The New Yorker magazine – September 21, 1981
"Hempstead County is a gently rolling countryside of fields and woods and brushy creeks."

Excerpted from *U.S. News & World Report* issue of July 11, 1983. Copyright 1983, U.S. News & World Report, Inc.
"What draws people to these hills is their wild beauty."

SPREAD NINE

Newsweek magazine – March 23, 1983
"The Thorncrown Chapel is the most striking example of what might be called the 'New Age of Metaphysical Architecture' in this country."

Reprinted from *Architectural Record* – February 1982. Copyright 1982, McGraw-Hill, Inc.
"The Mid-America Center serves a wide geographic area and serves it well. The building's lively forms arouse continuing interest, and its displays are expected to attract about a million visitors this year."

Town & Country magazine – November 1984
"Across the street is the 100-year-old Capital Hotel – a Victorian extravaganza complete with cast-iron front, solid brass railing, marbleized columns and the original stained-glass skylight."

SPREAD TEN

North American Hunter – Minneapolis, July/August 1982
"The huge rice-growing, green timber area attracts more ducks, and particularly mallards, than any place on the Mississippi Flyway, providing a duck hunting bonanza of magnificent quality and tremendous proportions."

SPREAD ELEVEN

Helen A. Wernle, *Endless Vacation* magazine – August 1985
"Few states celebrate fall with the verve of Arkansas. There, the fall calendar is peppered with festivals. Many are tied to the harvest season and the state's strong folk roots, and all add spice to the vacationer's agenda – spice that gives visitors the full flavor of Arkansas' heritage: A heritage of Indians, explorers, settlers and immigrants. A heritage that modern Arkansans proudly preserve and eagerly share."

SPREAD TWELVE

SPREAD THIRTEEN

SPREAD FOURTEEN

Now you know that Arkansas is one of the most photogenic states in America. We hope these sights have piqued your interest and told you more about Arkansas. Below, we add to your knowledge by identifying the photographs and telling something about the scene.

The pictures are identified in two-page spreads, with the descriptions beginning with the upper lefthand photograph and following clockwise around the two facing pages.

If you want to know more about the subject or location of one of these special Arkansas visions, just contact:
Arkansas Department of Parks and Tourism One Capitol Mall Little Rock, Arkansas 72201

ON THE COVER
This is Arkansas. Everywhere you look, every time you look, you discover something new about The Natural State. This book is your introduction to Arkansas. It is also your personal invitation to visit our state at every opportunity.

INSIDE FRONT COVER
The Ozarks share their secrets with those who are willing to walk a few miles and climb a mountain just to stand on the edge of tomorrow. This view from Whitaker Point is just one example.

PAGE ONE
Tucked away in the mountains of Arkansas are countless places where water cascades from one ledge to the next in stair-step waterfalls.

SPREAD ONE
This scene is from the top of White Rock Mountain near Ozark and Mulberry and is typical of many vistas throughout the Ozark and Ouachita Mountains.

The Spring River near Hardy is formed by the flow of Mammoth Spring and provides excellent canoeing and trout fishing.

The Goat Trail high above the Buffalo National River gives a unique perspective to Ozark scenery.

Pinnacle Mountain rises high above the Arkansas River Valley near Little Rock and provides a natural skyscraper for the capital city.

Massive and magnificent formations fill the underground wonderland in Blanchard Springs Caverns near Mountain View.

SPREAD TWO
The mountainside Victorian village of Eureka Springs takes on added beauty during the Ozarks' Flaming Fall Revue.

One waterfall leads to another in the Ouachita National Forest in southwest Arkansas near Glenwood.

The rice fields of eastern Arkansas stretch for miles across the delta. This is the world's largest rice field near Jonesboro.

The Buffalo National River of the Ozarks was the first stream in America to be designated as a National River.

Dogwoods bloom in all corners of The Natural State and put on a showy display along with the redbuds in March and April.

Old Washington State Park near Hope was the Confederate capital of Arkansas and the birthplace of the Bowie Knife.

SPREAD THREE
The world-famous White River flows clean, clear and cold from below Bull Shoals Dam providing the perfect home for rainbow, brown and cutthroat trout.

Island camping on Lake Ouachita is the ultimate way to leave the work-a-day world behind and enjoy the great outdoors.

The Arkansas River flows from west to east across the entire state and provides some of Arkansas' best bass fishing.

SPREAD FOUR
Little Rock, as seen from North Little Rock, as dusk settles on the Arkansas River.

Edwardian, Victorian and antebellum homes line the streets in the historic old river town of Helena.

The Crescent Hotel in Eureka Springs is the grand old hotel of the Ozarks and is listed on the National Register of Historic Places.

Historic Bathhouse Row in Hot Springs National Park is one of Arkansas' most familiar and treasured landmarks.

SPREAD FIVE

Scenic Highway 12 runs east out of Rogers and crosses the sparkling water of Beaver Lake.

Scenic Highway 7, which connects Russellville with Bull Shoals Lake, has been called one of the 10 most scenic drives in the United States.

An early spring drive along Highway 5 in north Lonoke County shows new buds on the trees and plenty of dogwood blossoms.

This covered bridge is in Burns Park in North Little Rock. The lake is for handicapped anglers only.

Looking east from a mountainside near Hot Springs, this view shows U.S. Highway 70 cutting through the Ouachita Mountains in autumn.

This bridge spans the mighty Mississippi River at Helena, a spot Mark Twain called ". . . one of the prettiest situations on the river."

SPREAD SIX

An evening at the Arkansas Arts Center can be entertaining, enlightening and is always enjoyable.

The Main Gallery of the Arkansas Arts Center features an ever-changing display of some of the finest works of art.

Major international artists perform in Little Rock and other Arkansas cities on a regular basis.

The University of Arkansas' Museum houses many outstanding artifacts. This one is known as "Big Boy." It is made of native bauxite and is considered one of the most valuable pieces in the collection.

SPREAD SEVEN

The Arkansas Symphony is recognized as one of the finest orchestras in the South.

Arkansas Rep, Little Rock's repertory theatre, stages many delightful productions each year.

The Saunders Memorial Museum in Berryville houses one of the world's largest collections of firearms featuring guns owned by the famous and the infamous.

SPREAD EIGHT

The Grand Canyon of the Ozarks stretches for miles. This view is looking east off Scenic Highway 7 just a few miles south of Jasper.

SPREAD NINE

Thorncrown Chapel is located just off Highway 62 east of Eureka Springs. This nondenominational chapel is open to the public at no charge.

Mid-America Museum at Hot Springs explores the principles of science and visitors work the exhibits in this unique hands-on museum.

The beautifully-restored Capital Hotel in downtown Little Rock is a fine example of the pride Arkansas has in its past.

SPREAD TEN

Arkansas duck hunters eagerly await those cold winter mornings when mallards come in on whistling wings.

SPREAD ELEVEN

The original Ozark Folk Festival is celebrated each fall in Eureka Springs and the whole town turns out for the celebration.

The Great Passion Play at Eureka Springs has been seen by well over three million people and has been called America's number one outdoor drama.

Quilting is just one of the many native crafts demonstrated daily at the Ozark Folk Center.

This diamond is from Crater of Diamonds State Park, the only diamond-producing field in North America. Visitors may keep any diamonds they find.

At the Ozark Folk Center just north of Mountain View, the music of the hills is passed down from one generation to the next.

SPREAD TWELVE

From February through mid-April, the excitement runs high in Hot Springs National Park. This is the time of year for the Oaklawn race meet which attracts the nation's top horses, jockeys and trainers to the spa city. Oaklawn is ranked as one of America's finest race tracks.

When the beloved "Hogs" hit the field at Little Rock's War Memorial Stadium, there's never an empty seat.

Razorback fans of all ages go hog wild for the athletic teams of the University of Arkansas at Fayetteville.

Southland Greyhound Park at West Memphis is rated as one of America's finest greyhound racing facilities.

SPREAD THIRTEEN

Hikers stroll along the narrow ledge called the Goat Trail high above the Buffalo River near Ponca.

The crystal clear waters of Lake Ouachita have earned it the title of one of the two cleanest lakes in America.

Most Arkansas lakes are clear and clean and attract scuba divers from all over the country.

The setting sun seems to sit atop Pinnacle Mountain as its golden rays are reflected in the Arkansas River at Little Rock.

Small, unnamed streams and springs abound in Arkansas and eventually provide us with 9,700 miles of streams and rivers and 600,000 acres of lakes.

The Spring River below Mammoth Spring and down to Hardy is an excellent place for novice canoeists to develop their skills.

A ride down the roaring waters of the Buffalo National River is an exhilarating experience. The best floating is in early spring.

SPREAD FOURTEEN

"Granny's Attic" in the Old State House, Arkansas' first capitol, provides youngsters with a glimpse of life in a bygone day.

The Little Red River flows from below Greers Ferry Dam near Heber Springs, making a fine home for fighting rainbow trout.

Early morning mists shroud the White River as anglers wait for the first trout of the day to strike.

The main dining room of the Governor's Mansion is the scene of many official dinners and receptions. The Mansion is located in Little Rock's Quapaw Quarter.

Wild River Country at North Little Rock is a water theme park where kids of all ages can be as relaxed or as daring as they wish.

Arkansas has plenty of huge impoundments where the wind fills the sails, and boats skim across the water.

Natural Dam on Lee Creek just north of Van Buren is a swimming hole made-to-order by Mother Nature.

This field of wildflowers happens to be near Mena but the scene is a common sight throughout the Ouachita Mountains.

Natural Bridge, just off Highway 65 north of Clinton, shows the wonders worked by the forces of nature.

Someone will have to point the way to Lost Valley in Buffalo River Country, but it's worth asking about and worth the walk.

The individuals who responded to Governor Clinton's invitation to underwrite the Sesquicentennial Celebration defy any generalized description. Though they share some common characteristics, they are a diverse lot in background, style and the ways they make a living. It would be unfair to many others, not to mention being grossly inaccurate, to imply that these are the only preeminent leaders in the Arkansas business community. Such a list would be much longer. The ones who chose to help, however, while not necessarily representative in terms of race, sex, region or all of Arkansas's economy, are an unquestionably distinguished group. Each has a record of excellence in the business and civic arenas.

The Southwestern Bell Foundation made a contribution to the Sesquicentennial with the stipulation that its pages in this book be devoted to honoring Dr. Bessie Boehm Moore. As an advocate of education and other causes, Dr. Moore has devoted her life and intellect to pursuits which have not made her a fortune but have contributed generously to the quality of life in Arkansas and the nation.

The limitations of space necessarily restricted the breadth of these articles, which are intended to offer at least a bare outline of how each individual attained his or her level of success. Short of detailed biographies, however, it is nearly impossible to do justice to the contributions these leaders have made to the wellbeing of this state. Brevity also makes it difficult to depict adequately the role played in their lives by such qualities as perseverance, vision and ingenuity.

It ought to be noted at this point that a scant few of the Sesquicentennial Sponsors were born to any appreciable measure of family wealth. On the contrary, several are the offspring of families which lived at the economic edge of existence. And even those few born to relative affluence have fashioned their own destinies. They are making their mark in the world and surely would have regardless of the material circumstances of their birth.

The Great Depression left an indelible mark on most of them. The Arkansas economy was fairly lackluster even before the stock market crash in 1929, especially in the hill country where many families barely forced a subsistence living out of the rocky soil. In the 1930's, times got a lot harder. Several Sponsors reached adulthood in the midst of the Depression; others spent their childhood in those trying years.

Whatever their origins, the Sponsors are individuals who have created for themselves, their families and thousands of employees an economic lot far better than they were accustomed to as children. And they have done so in a variety of endeavors that offer an interesting sampling of Arkansas business. They have been innovative and, most of them, rather daring, sometimes risking about everything they had in pursuit of an idea.

Some of these individuals at one time or another swam against the current, ignoring popular trends and plunging headlong into an enterprise with a singular confidence that they were guided by foresight.

Doc Toland got into the wholesale grocery business at a time when many assumed that the great food-store chains would continue to dominate the market. He participated in reversing that trend.

Jerry Jones became fascinated with oil and gas exploration at a time when it was in decline and others were leaving the business. He got into the field just ahead of the greatest explosion in energy prices in history. When prices plunged following that boom, Jones again pursued an independent course by continuing exploration when the trend in this country was to leave the field.

Don Munro, faced with the invasion of foreign-made shoes, could have tucked tail and run. Not only has he continued manufacturing footwear exclusively in the United States, but he has expanded his operations even as the market share for American-made shoes was shrinking.

Just a look at their titles suggests that each of the Sponsors could formulate and pursue a dream. Even more fascinating is the degree to which some in particular could work toward a distant goal with no significant intermediate rewards. Jerry Maulden had too many mouths to feed to go to college full time. It took eight and a half years of night classes and more than one job at a time for him to earn his degree. He never faltered. J.B. Hunt was sure that he could come up with a machine to pack wood shavings for chicken houses. He tinkered with the design of the device for 15 years before it was patented. By then, it was to pack rice hulls. It was that machine which eventually helped provide him and Johnelle the financial base to launch their immensely successful trucking company.

William Dillard tells his story so matter-of-factly that from the tone of the tale, you wouldn't think it was anything out of the ordinary. In the interview, he started out saying, "I was born in Mineral Springs." An hour later, after he had made the development of the nation's largest department store company sound like simply a

85

few good rolls on a Monopoly board, he ended just as plainly. "And that's the story of my life," he said.

Dillard's father must have had a pretty good notion of how well his son could stretch a dollar. When he left the young Dillard at Fayetteville to go to college, he gave him a checkbook and told him to use what he needed. He never had occasion to complain about the draws on the account. Later, William Dillard did the same for his children, though he was able to do it with a largess his father surely could not have imagined.

Old-timers in Arkansas used to say you could throw up a wall around the state, and it would survive. These latter-day entrepreneurs, fortunately, have a much broader perspective. The businesses of a majority of them are at least national in scope.

Several of the Sponsors do business internationally. When Richard Bell was interviewed, he was fretting about a $4 million load of Riceland rice sitting in a ship in a Turkish harbor. The Turks hadn't approved the unloading yet. The ultimate destination of the rice was Iraq. Charles Cella, king of horse racing in Arkansas, manufactures log homes that are sold internationally. Jack Stephens has extensive holdings in the Far East and is involved in international trade. Peterson Industries, Inc., supplies poultry breeding stock to 40 foreign countries.

The interrelationships of many of these businesses in the marketplace are interesting, especially in the food industry. Nobody gets more excited in talking about competition than Jerry Hamra, also known as "Mr. Wendy's." Hamra's philosophy is that "there will always be a place for a good hamburger." He speaks kindly of the Number One fast-food chain and appears to feast on the challenge of the competition. What the average customer may not realize is that Hamra competes with more than other restaurants. He's also butting heads with the grocers—like Affiliated Foods—and the producers of prepared foods for the home—like Hudson Foods. Americans are starting to eat at home more than they were for a few years. Hamra has to come up with imaginative ways to get them into his restaurants.

Riceland is challenging the potato in the realm of staples and is doing an increasing restaurant business. However, their grand plan includes carving out a larger share of the market in prepared foods for the hurried and harried in the home. They aim to convince people to stay at home for more meals by offering a broader array of rice-based dishes that can be prepared in a matter of minutes.

Many of the Sponsors place special emphasis on the importance of their employees. Munro & Company developed an employee life-fitness program more than a decade ago that continues to grow and attract wider participation. Hamra stresses the importance of regular contact with workers in all 20 of his stores. Sam Walton, founder of Wal-Mart Stores, Inc., insists that his employees be called "associates," and he knows thousands of them by name.

J.B. and Johnelle Hunt spend a lot of time in the air making frequent visits to all seven of their terminals across the country. Every day that he is at the home office at Lowell, it is a morning ritual for J.B. to do a walk-through to greet and, usually, touch as many employees as possible. When they travel by car, they eat at truck stops where they can visit with their drivers.

Perhaps it should go without saying, but the Sponsors are bullish on Arkansas. They are here by choice. Several whose enterprises are spread around the country could have headquarters elsewhere.

Most of them listed "quality of life" as the state's most marketable asset in the highly competitive game of attracting new business to Arkansas. At the same time, several of them expressed concern that in the rush to greater economic development the state should take care not to diminish that quality.

Herschel Friday feels that one of the most attractive features of Arkansas is its size. You can know so many people that it makes practicing law or doing business of any kind easier, he says.

Herbert McAdams II is an advocate of personal contact in economic development, and he probably has done as much of that as anyone in Arkansas. He argues that there is no substitute for getting to know people in business around the country, then asking them to locate in your community or state.

"We ought to do better than we do in Arkansas," McAdams says, "because it's easier."

McAdams and the rest of these leaders have found it easier to live in Arkansas, easier to work in Arkansas and easier to grow in Arkansas. They are among the state's staunchest advocates.

Their stories, presented on the following pages, tell a lot about Arkansas.

The Anthony Family

Oliver Anthony (upper left), John William Anthony, Garland Anthony and Frank Anthony / South Arkansas

The Anthony name has been synonymous with the forestry industry in Arkansas since early in this century. Today, one branch of the family claims a United States Congressman, while another has title to one of the largest privately owned lumber companies in the South.

The Arkansas roots of the family go back to about 1840, when Adderson Anthony settled in the Freeo Creek bottom in northwest Calhoun County. His origins are unknown. Family lore has it that he rode into the creek bottom on a beautiful horse, built his log cabin far back in the woods and never received a visitor or a piece of mail from his past associations. Adderson supposedly had some money and at least a little education. The land he settled has remained in the family and belongs now to a great-grandson.

Adderson's son, John Franklin Anthony, had 12 children. His four sons—Oliver (1878-1954), John William (1882-1958), Garland (1884-1981) and Frank (1890-1970)—would later make the Anthony family a major force in the forestry industry in Arkansas, Texas and Louisiana.

John Franklin was a farmer and a merchant and, with a brother, Jule, operated sawmills near Hopeville. They were seasonal operations. The four brothers began learning the business at these little

mills. In 1907, one was located on a Cotton Belt Railroad siding near Bearden known as Harlow. From this point forward, the family was always in the lumber business.

John Franklin left sawmilling to return to the farm, but the four brothers continued to run mills of small size until they formed Anthony Brothers Lumber Company and built their first large mill at Hopeville in 1930. This mill could produce 10 million board feet of lumber a year.

Garland, Will, Oliver and Frank were enterprising and aggressive lumbermen. From the time they built the original Hopeville mill until the 1950's, they operated numerous sawmills through partnerships or as individual ventures. Some of John Franklin's sons-in-law were also in the lumber business, both individually and as partners with the four brothers.

In the heyday of their operations in the 1930's and 1940's, the Anthonys had as many as 25 mills in operation simultaneously. Garland Anthony, through a network of partnerships with various combinations of brothers and brothers-in-law, was at one time reputed to be the largest independent lumber producer in the world.

By the 1950's, the partnerships began to dissolve, and the family holdings became centered in three distinct groups. Frank Anthony and

his children had Anthony Forest Products Company, headquartered at El Dorado with mills in Arkansas, Texas and Louisiana. Will Anthony and his family had formed the Murfreesboro Lumber Company with several mills in the state. Garland and Oliver Anthony and their families had centralized their Arkansas operations in the Bearden Lumber Company, located about two miles from Harlow. They also operated mills in Vidor, Newton and Woodville, Texas.

Murfreesboro Lumber Company was sold to Weyerhaeuser in 1977.

Anthony Forest Products now has two sawmills, one in Urbana, Arkansas, and another in Atlanta, Texas, and two laminating plants, with 40,000 acres in three states. The company also has farming operations in Miller County, Arkansas. The company president is Beryl Anthony Sr., one of Frank's sons and the father of United States Representative Beryl Anthony Jr.

Anthony Timberlands, Inc., of Bearden, operates the Bearden Lumber Company in Bearden and mills at Malvern and Beirne, Arkansas, and is headed by John E. Anthony, Garland's grandson. With 125,000 acres of timberland, they produce 160,000,000 board feet of lumber annually, making them one of the largest privately owned lumber companies in the South.

Melvyn Bell

Chairman of the Board and Chief Executive Officer / Environmental Systems Company (ENSCO) / Little Rock, Arkansas

Melvyn Bell is a man of broad and contrasting interests. In his management of Environmental Systems Company (ENSCO), he is as modern as tomorrow's technology. Elsewhere, he manifests a costly devotion to preservation. And some of his investments are for just plain fun.

Bell is best known as the chairman of the board and chief executive officer of ENSCO, one of the leading companies in the United States in the disposal of hazardous wastes.

In recent years, however, he has expanded his personal investments into theme parks, resorts, radio stations, restaurants, lumber companies, retail antiques and four of the bathhouses on Bathhouse Row in Hot Springs.

Long ago Bell developed a knack for taking businesses that were on the ropes, injecting a lot of energy, innovation and good management into them and turning them around. He has also invested with an eye to furthering his interests in the economic development of Arkansas and preserving relics of the past.

Bell, a native of Fort Smith, received his Bachelor of Science in Electrical Engineering Degree in 1960 from the University of Arkansas at Fayetteville.

From 1960 to 1969, he was a principal in Mickle-Bell Associates, Consulting Engineers, of Fort Smith, where he was involved in water, sewer and solid-waste disposal projects. In 1969, he became a co-founder and general manager of Bell-Burrough-Uerline-Brausell, another consulting engineering firm.

By 1972 Bell had become an investor in ENSCO because of his growing interest in waste-disposal technology. ENSCO was not faring so well at the time, which made it the kind of situation which unfailingly attracts Bell's attention. He bought his partners out that year and launched a period of growth that shows no signs of abating yet.

In 1981, ENSCO earned a federal permit to incinerate hazardous waste, a procedure that has become the company's specialty and its salvation. Revenues had risen to $66.5 million by 1987. Bell has set a goal of $1 billion in income by 1995.

The company is now a recognized pioneer in the field of waste disposal. Besides operating large permanently-installed incinerators, ENSCO has lead the development of portable modular units.

Through an aggressive program of applied research, ENSCO is looking at other technologies to be used instead of or in conjunction with incineration. At the same time, Bell expects to continue improving the incineration process and its production of usable by-products, such as steam for generating electricity.

He is intrigued by the possibility of generating at least 1 per cent of nation's electricity needs through the incineration of all garbage and chemical wastes.

Discovering and developing potentials is a characteristic of Bell's style, not only in investments and development of markets, but in his selection of personnel. If he finds a talented, hard-working individual, he generally hires the person, regardless of whether he has a specific job in mind at the time. He also believes in sharing the rewards. Many of his key people have significant stock positions in ENSCO.

Perhaps the most tangible demonstration yet of his commitment to the development of talent, as well as the development of Arkansas, was his donation of $8 million for the construction of a new engineering building at the University of Arkansas.

He is also deeply interested in the development of a high-technology corridor between Little Rock and Pine Bluff.

"But it will only happen if we make it happen," Bell says.

Richard Bell

President and Chief Executive Officer / Riceland Foods, Inc. / Stuttgart, Arkansas

Arkansas is the nation's leading rice producer, and Richard Bell, president of Riceland Foods, Inc., is the state's major rice promoter.

Bell is an Illinois boy by birth, but he has been gone from the Midwest a long time. He came to Arkansas by way of Maryland, Canada, Belgium, Ireland and Washington, D.C.

"We haven't been disappointed," Bell says of the decision he and his wife and two sons made in 1977 to move to the Arkansas Grand Prairie.

After nearly 18 years with the United States Department of Agriculture, the last two years as the third ranking officer in the agency, Bell left federal service at the dawn of the Carter Administration. He was on the verge of accepting an offer in Stamford, Connecticut, when L. C. Carter, then president of Riceland Foods of Stuttgart, invited him to Arkansas.

The visit led to a job offer. Finding small-town life appealing, Bell's family concurred, and he became executive vice president and chief operating officer of Riceland. In 1981, the Riceland Board of Directors elected him president and chief executive officer.

In 1987 Arkansas farmers produced 120 million bushels of rice—40 per cent of the nation's production—and 62.4 million of those bushels were processed by Riceland. In addition, another 72 million bushels of other grains went through the Riceland system.

Riceland sells more than half its grain to foreign markets.

International trade has interested Bell since he was in high school in Clinton, Illinois, where he grew up on a corn, soybean and livestock farm. Having already decided by then against being a farmer—he wanted to see the world—Bell went to the University of Illinois at Urbana and earned his bachelor's and master's degrees in agricultural economics.

After a year on the staff at the University of Maryland, he signed on with the Agriculture Department as an agricultural economist. Two years later, he started seeing more of the world. Between 1961 and 1965, he worked as assistant agricultural attache in the United States embassies at Ottawa and Brussels. From 1965 to 1968, he was agricultural attache at the embassy in Dublin.

Returning to Washington, he became chief of foreign grain marketing in the Agriculture Department, later director of the Grain Division of the Department's Foreign Agricultural Service, then a deputy assistant secretary, and, finally, assistant secretary of agriculture. In the latter position, Bell was a political appointee. He even did some campaigning in farm areas for then President Gerald R. Ford—his only fling at campaign politics.

Although he had never been in Arkansas before 1977, Bell had become acquainted with L.C. Carter during the early 1970's. Working at the time on new rice legislation, Bell called on Carter to enlist the legislative support of the late Senator John L. McClellan. They were successful in Congress, and Carter remembered Bell several years later when he was seeking a possible successor to his position at Riceland.

Riceland and Bell have been a lucrative match. Sales in 1986 were $530 million. Riceland has 2,200 employees and, while continuing its massive export program, the company is moving aggressively into new domestic markets.

Domestic marketing offers an exciting challenge and an attractive alternative to international sales. This burgeoning market has the potential of significantly improving the lot of Arkansas rice farmers. Value-added products, those prepared for sale to consumers, are more profitable for Riceland. And that translates to more profits for the farmers, who own the giant cooperative.

Charles J. Cella

Chairman of the Board / Oaklawn Jockey Club / Hot Springs National Park, Arkansas

Charles J. Cella has a passion for theater and thoroughbred racing. He brings some of the theater to his racetrack and makes Oaklawn Jockey Club at Hot Springs the state's top tourist attraction.

"I operate this racetrack not as a business but as a paramour," Cella says, explaining that some costly frills are not profitable but enhance the atmosphere of entertainment at the track.

Consider those mammoth Clydesdales which tow the starting gate into position. They bestow a touch of powerful pageantry, but they cost Cella $200,000 a year. And there is no hard evidence to suggest that they garner so much as an additional dollar in revenues. A tractor would suffice—and does when the weather is bad.

"We've always believed in tradition at this track," Cella says, "and we have a certain style that is seductive . . . We cater to the entertainment world more than to the gambling."

Entertainment of one kind or another has been the focus of the Cella family for at least three generations.

"We're the oldest family in American theater and the oldest family in horse racing," Cella says.

His grandfather built many of the Orpheum theaters in the heyday of vaudeville. In the same era, Grandfather Cella and his brothers, whom Cella calls "the Cella Boys," operated off-track betting shops when they were legal in Missouri. Then the Cella Boys decided that the real money was in owning the racetracks, which they set about doing with such elan that within a decade, they owned most of the tracks in North America. That included Oaklawn's predecessor, Essex Park, whose vague outlines are still visible in the shallow waters of Lake Catherine. A tornado destroyed Essex Park in 1903, but the Cella Boys opened Oaklawn a year later. After an on-again, off-again history of being legalized one year and outlawed another, the track finally closed down in 1919, and it looked like forever.

In 1934, however, at the invitation of Hot Springs officials and business leaders, Cella's grandfather reopened Oaklawn. Thoroughbreds have raced in Arkansas ever since.

Cella's father took over the track on the death of his father in 1942 and ran it until his own death in 1968. Then the Oaklawn Jockey Club passed to Charles Cella.

Cella did not set out as a young man to run a racetrack. When he received his Bachelor of Science Degree from Washington and Lee University at Lexington, Virginia, he enrolled in the Northwestern University School of Law at Evanston, Illinois. Before classes started, Cella's father summoned him home to help with the family's theater business. Cella went home expecting to be in a management position in their theater chain, but he found himself making $42 a week doing all kinds of things for his father. One week, after a production of "My Fair Lady" had been a box-office flop, he didn't even get the $42.

Today, Cella is chief executive of three other businesses besides Oaklawn: American Theatrical Company of St. Louis, Southern Real Estate and Financial Company (developer of University Mall at Little Rock) and Town and Country Log Homes of Petoskey, Michigan.

For a number of years, Cella served on the board of directors of First National Bank of Little Rock (now First Commercial Bank). He was one of the founders and is a former board member of Hot Springs Savings and Loan Association. He has served on the board of the National Gypsum Corporation, a worldwide building materials and products manufacturer and distributor. He is a trustee of the Eye Retina Foundation of Boston, the world's largest independent eye research center for the prevention of blindness and other eye disease.

J.D. Cobb

Planter / Keo, Arkansas

The first J.D. Cobb settled in the area around Keo in the hardest of times. It was 1864 when he moved there from Rome, Georgia, in the waning days of the Civil War. He started out sharecropping, but within a few years he had made the difficult transition to farming and ginning on his own. Today, his grandson, the second J.D. Cobb, carries on a tradition that has persisted even into the fourth generation of the family.

At one time there was a Cobbs, Arkansas, with its own post office. Then the railroad came through nearby Keo, and the Cobbs and everybody else followed the rails.

Cobb lives in Keo and oversees the operation of a 4,400-acre farm producing cotton, soybeans, rice, wheat and pecans. He also owns a general store at Keo, and his son and a partner run the family cotton gin.

The land in eastern Pulaski County and Lonoke County, where the Cobb farm lies, looks now as if it had always been clear and cultivated. A century ago, however, Cobb's forbears found most of it still in hardwood forests and cypress swamps.

By the turn of the century, when Samuel C. Cobb, Cobb's father, started farming and ginning, many of the swamps remained. Cobb remembers the sawmill his father had on the back of a cypress brake. It was powered by a steam engine that ran the sawmill in the spring and summer and the gin in the winter.

"I used to like to blow the whistle," Cobb recalls.

Early in this century, large-scale construction of canals drained most of the remaining swamps. By the time Cobb was grown, the land was about as open as it is today.

Cobb was born about a mile and a half away from his present home in Keo, one of only three children in his family to live beyond infancy. The first five babies born to the Samuel Cobbs died. When J.D. Cobb was five, the family moved into a rambling red-brick house, which still stands today across the road from the handsome buff brick Cobb built in 1939, a year after his marriage.

After his graduation from England High School, Cobb enrolled in what is now Ouachita Baptist University at Arkadelphia, where he received a Bachelor of Arts Degree in economics in 1932. That fall he began graduate work at the University of Texas at Austin, leaving two years later lacking only six hours of Texas history to earn a master's degree.

On his return to Arkansas, Cobb followed in the footsteps of his father and grandfather and took up farming. In those days they relied heavily on sharecroppers, two families to every 40 acres. Today, there are none. When Cobb started out, they picked cotton all fall and into the winter. In the fall of 1986, his machines picked 4,000 bales of cotton in less than a month.

Back in 1918, Samuel Cobb began planting pecan trees, which are peculiarly adapted to the deep soil of that region. Most of the trees had died by the time J.D. Cobb came home from Austin. So he began replanting in 1935 and today has 2,400 pecan trees and a shelling and packing operation that prepares them for shipment all over the country.

His pecan grove stretches northward from Highway 165 at Keo with the grace and order of a classical garden.

Aside from his agricultural pursuits, Cobb serves on the boards of both J. B. Hunt Transport Services, Inc., of Lowell and Superior Federal Savings and Loan Company of Little Rock. He is a former member of the board of the Baptist Medical System and the school boards of both Keo and England.

Cobb is a deacon at the Keo Baptist Church.

John A. Cooper Sr.

Chairman of the Board / Cooper Communities, Inc. / Bentonville, Arkansas

After World War II the economy was in a lot better shape than it was in the 1930's, and Social Security was making it possible for more Americans to retire with a measure of dignity.

John A. Cooper Sr. was taking notes on this social phenomenon in the late 1940's and slowly putting together an idea for capitalizing on it.

"We did a study," he says, "and found that in a 500-mile radius, about every twelve seconds somebody was getting a gold watch."

Cooper surmised that a good number of those retirees might find the idea of a carefully planned retirement community appealing. He had been building subdivisions in established towns, but he believed that, properly marketed to older people, a totally new community could rise in a rural setting. He could pretty well build it anywhere, without the necessity of having industry and commerce nearby to provide jobs. What he needed was a vast tract of scenic land in the hill country to provide ample space for houses and the amenities of the good life in the country—fishing lakes, golf courses, tennis courts, country clubs.

Of course, such a radical departure from the conventional wisdom required a superior job of salesmanship,

and the first people he had to sell were the bankers and insurance companies, the potential financial backers of the venture. They didn't go for it right away.

"I ran the business two days and looked for credit for five days," Cooper said, recalling his many trips to St. Louis and, later, New York, in search of money to turn his dream into reality.

Cooper outlasted the resistance, however, and in 1952 he opened Cherokee Village in Northwest Arkansas, eventually acquiring 22,000 acres. In the meantime, he had hired Purdue University's first graduate in land planning. He meant to do it right.

Today, Cooper Communities, Inc., has three growing planned communities in Arkansas—Bella Vista opened in 1968 and Hot Springs Village in 1972—and four others outside the state.

The company is still wholly owned by the Cooper family, and he is chairman of the board. Although at 81 he has built thousands of retirement homes for others, he has not retired.

Every year, the Cooper Communities' nationwide marketing program brings about 100,000 visitors into Arkansas.

Cooper, who was born at Earle and grew up at Marion, did not set out to be

a land developer. He came into the real estate business from a side door during the ten years he practiced law as a young man.

He had taken a short-cut to law, studying first for a year at Washington and Lee University at Lexington, Virginia, then completing a one-year program at Cumberland University at Lebanon, Tennessee. That enabled him to pass the bar examination in 1927, but Cooper says now that the brevity of his training left him somewhat at a disadvantage.

If he was indeed at a disadvantage, he overcame it soon enough. By the time his law partner, E. C. (Took) Gathings, got elected to Congress in 1938, Cooper had dealt in real estate enough to know that it was much more suited to his tastes than the practice of law. So he took down his shingle.

By then he was doing drainage construction, and around the time the war started, he was building houses, which he has been doing ever since.

Cooper's idea for retirement communities attracted national attention and, as might be expected, drew a crowd of imitators. Today, there are many such planned communities both in rural and suburban environments.

William T. Dillard Sr.

Chairman of the Board / Dillard Department Stores / Little Rock, Arkansas

William T. Dillard Sr. kept a family tradition and became a retailer. His father had a general store at Mineral Springs, and his grandfather owned a store in another little town.

Dillard had a little store once upon a time. Today, he is chairman of the board of Dillard Department Stores, Inc., the leading department store company in America. Sales in 1986 approached $2 billion. By mid-year 1987, the company owned 117 stores in 11 states, with the end neither in sight nor planned.

When Dillard talks about his life and business, though, he makes it all sound much easier than it could possibly have been.

Born at Mineral Springs in Howard County, he finished high school when he was 16 years old and went up to Fayetteville to study accounting at the University of Arkansas. A superior academic record there paved the way to a scholarship at Columbia University in New York, where he received his master's degree in retailing in 1937. Then he entered management training at a Sears store in Tulsa, Oklahoma, the only time in his life when he worked for anyone besides his father or himself.

In 1938, with a cash investment of something less than $8,000, he opened Dillard's of Nashville, a dry-goods store that made a $3,000 profit on $42,000 in sales the first year. He sold the store in 1948 with enough money to buy half-interest in a much larger store in Texarkana. In 1956, he bought the largest department store in Tyler, Texas.

By 1960, Dillard really wanted to be in business in Little Rock, but opportunity presented itself in Tulsa. And it was the Tulsa experience which set the pace for what is still happening 28 years later. The financial magic he worked there has become something of a trademark for Dillard and has accounted for much of the growth since then.

What happened in Tulsa was that the largest department store in town was floundering, and four banks stood to lose several million dollars if it collapsed. After selling stock to some friends in Tyler, Dillard bought the store and, within a year, turned it around. Two of those grateful banks to this day participate in Dillard's lines of credit. Many of the stores the company owns today were losers bought from other companies and saved from failure.

Since the purchase of the Tulsa stores, Dillard has bought many other stores that were either unprofitable or, at best, marginal. His keys to rehabilitating these operations have included sound management, more and better sales personnel, quality merchandise and lots of it, and facelifts for older buildings.

In the early 1960's, Dillard tried to buy the Blass department store in Little Rock, in part because he wanted to base his operations in the capital city of his home state.

"But they wouldn't talk to me," he recalls, "so I bought Pfeifer's."

Pfeifer's of Arkansas was the city's other leading department store. Six months after Dillard took it over in 1963, Blass went on the market. Dillard didn't have the money to buy another big store so quickly. So he turned to a friend who owned a trading stamp company. He recalls the conversation:

"I said, 'George, if you'll come up here and pay for it for me, I'll give Green Stamps in Tulsa and Little Rock.' He was here the next day."

The Pfeifer's and Blass stores eventually were given the Dillard name. Today, the company is a strong presence in Arkansas with stores at Little Rock, North Little Rock, Texarkana, Jonesboro, Fayetteville, Fort Smith, Pine Bluff and Hot Springs.

The company made its first public offering of stock in 1968.

Herschel H. Friday

Senior Partner / Friday, Eldredge & Clark / Little Rock, Arkansas

The law firm of Friday, Eldredge & Clark of Little Rock has become an institution in Arkansas.

The Friday Firm, as it is commonly called, is the largest in Arkansas and counts among its clients the state's two largest utilities and largest railroad. Its origins go back to 1871.

When a book called "The Best Lawyers in America" was published in 1982, it cited Herschel H. Friday, the firm's senior partner, and five of his partners.

Lawyers from the Friday firm can be found in the leadership of professional associations and civic and religious endeavors. It is hard to find a major public issue that does not somehow involve the Friday Firm or its partners.

Friday is a former president of the Arkansas Bar Association and former member of the Board of Governors of the American Bar Association. For more than 30 years, he has been a member of the American Bar's House of Delegates.

He has served on the Board of Directors of the Arkansas Children's Hospital and as chairman of the Development Council of the University of Arkansas at Little Rock. He is also chairman of the UALR Board of Visitors.

In the business world, Friday is a member of the boards of directors of the First Commercial Corporation, the Oaklawn Jockey Club, Inc., Southwestern Bell Corporation and Great Lakes Chemical Corporation.

Friday sees his and his partners' involvement in community life as being fitting in view of the success they have enjoyed professionally.

"I owe something to the community," he says.

Today, Friday is one of Arkansas' most prominent citizens, with the list of his associations and honors running to several pages. He didn't come in to this world, however, with any of the trappings of social prominence.

Born in 1922 in Sevier County, he learned as a child what it was to be poor. In the midst of the Depression, his family moved to Little Rock, where his father went to work for the state Highway Department. Friday had already decided by then that he wanted to be a lawyer.

After high school, Friday enrolled at what is now the University of Arkansas at Little Rock, then later transferred to the Fayetteville campus, doggedly pursuing his dream of studying law.

World War II interrupted his education for three years during which he was a pilot in the Air Force. After his discharge, he went right back to school and finally earned his law degree and admission to practice in 1947.

One of his professors helped him become law clerk to the late Federal Judge John Miller of Fort Smith, an appointment which Friday credits for much of his success in private practice.

In 1952, Friday joined the firm he has been with ever since.

He is married to the former Nancy Elizabeth Hammett.

Among the honors he has received over the years are these:

- Outstanding Lawyer Award of 1971 by the Arkansas Bar Association.
- Shield of the Trojan Award of 1976 by the University of Arkansas at Little Rock.
- Arkansas March of Dimes Citizen of the Year of 1981.
- UALR Builders Award of 1983.

One of Friday's current interests is raising funds for establishment of a permanent home for the Arkansas Repertory Theatre.

"We owe it to our community to have the broadest possible cultural advantages available to our people and those that are coming in here," Friday says. "You won't attract investment without it."

Gerald F. (Jerry) Hamra

Chairman of the Board and Chief Executive Officer / Wendy's of Little Rock / North Little Rock, Arkansas

Gerald F. (Jerry) Hamra had the best of times and the worst of times as a child growing up in Steele, Missouri, during the Great Depression.

By the time Jerry was born in 1930, Sam Hamra, his father, was well established in the dry-goods business.

Tragedy struck in 1936 when Jerry fell victim to polio, the scourge of childhood back then. The disease crippled both legs badly and kept him out of school for a full year. Even though the elder Hamra was able to secure the best care available, treatment of polio in those days was rather primitive. Jerry spent long periods in the hospital. When he was 13 years old, he had three major operations. Those procedures and a brace made life in his adolescent years fairly normal.

In spite of the disease, Hamra began working in the family department store as a child and learned enough to run the business in later years.

The department store closed its doors in 1984, finally succumbing to the dwindling population of the farm country in the Missouri Bootheel.

Now, Hamra sells hamburgers, among other things, and harbors no notions of going back into what he calls "the rag business."

Since 1975, he has opened 20 Wendy's restaurants in Arkansas and carved out a growing share of the fiercely competitive fast-food market.

By the time Hamra discovered Wendy's and opened his first franchised restaurant in Kansas City in January 1975, he already had a discouraging track record with franchises. He had been involved with two different parent companies which went broke and took his franchised stores under with them.

Undaunted, he and a cousin bought the franchise rights for Wendy's stores in Kansas City and Central Arkansas. They were convinced that Wendy's was financially sound and in the business for the long haul.

When the Kansas City operation got underway profitably, the cousins opened their first Arkansas store in December 1975 in North Little Rock.

As both businesses grew, Hamra and his cousin traded out. The cousin took the Missouri stores, and Hamra got the Arkansas operations.

Hamra's management style is intensely personal. He is known for working long hours and takes great pride in getting around to every one of his 20 restaurants at least every two weeks. He is a perfectionist who demands from his more than 1,000 employees attention to detail, cleanliness and friendly service.

Persistence has paid off. Not only has Wendy's taken Hamra and his family beyond the relative affluence of his childhood, but it has enabled him to become a prominent philanthropist. Maybe it's the weakened leg on which he wears a permanent brace, maybe it's just the memories of endless days in the hospital, but most of his charitable work benefits children.

In recognition of his generous support, the Arkansas Children's Hospital, in 1985, named its new rehabilitation center in his honor. His response was to raise the money to build a $300,000 therapeutic pool for the center.

Wendy's of Little Rock was the first franchise group in the country to receive the "Wendy's International Founder's Award," which cited Hamra's operation as "a lesson in quality and management—a prototype for others to emulate." The following year, the Little Rock group received the "Wendy's Award," thus becoming the only franchise in the country to receive both honors.

In November 1985, Hamra received "The Promethean Award" from the March of Dimes.

In 1987, Wendy's was recognized as "Business of the Year" in North Little Rock, where the company maintains its headquarters.

James T. (Red) Hudson

Chairman of the Board / Hudson Foods, Inc. / Rogers, Arkansas

James T. (Red) Hudson finished high school at Tyler, Tennessee, when the country was about halfway through World War II. Like many another 17-year-old then, he signed up and went off to fight the war.

When he came home three years later, Hudson took a $32-a-week job as a clerk in a Ralston-Purina feed store. Over the next 26 years, he worked his way up the Ralston-Purina corporate ladder.

At one point, Hudson was over all of the Ralston-Purina feed stores. When the poultry industry began the move toward vertical integration—that is, expansion into all levels from breeding to processing—he was one of the company's leading advocates of the change and helped accomplish it. Finally, he ended up at Rogers, Arkansas, as the head of one of Ralston-Purina's five regional poultry operations.

When Hudson sensed that the company wasn't too keen on keeping its poultry division—"it didn't fit their scheme of things," he says—he put together a plan to buy the operation he was running. The negotiations with Ralston-Purina were long and at times seemingly futile and took 120 days before an agreement was reached.

Hudson finally prevailed and, in February 1972,

made the purchase and named the new company Hudson Foods, Inc.

To finance the purchase, Hudson persuaded two competitors to sign bank notes in return for stock. Eventually, he bought their stock back, and in 1986, he made his first public stock offering, while retaining the majority of the shares.

The public offering had some historical significance in financial circles. Hudson says his was the first "chicken company" in about 25 years to go public, and it took some talking to educate the New York underwriters. The venture was highly successful, and three other companies have followed suit since then.

Sales the first year of operation were $32 million. In the fiscal year ending September 1986, Hudson Foods had sales of $225 million. In fiscal 1987, sales jumped to $428.9 million.

Hudson has been buying smaller companies and expects to continue these acquisitions in keeping with a national trend in an industry where the top ten companies control about 80 per cent of the sales volume. Hudson is now ranked seventh in the nation.

"We're either going to have to acquire or be acquired," he says, leaving no doubt that he has opted for the former.

Total employment at Hudson Foods is now more than 5,000. Another 2,000 independent contractors—about half of them in the Arkansas-Missouri area—raise Hudson chickens on their farms.

Presently, a little more than half of the company's chicken products and about 45 per cent of its turkeys go out under the Hudson Foods label. Hudson's goal is to have it all under the house label.

Another goal is to reach a billion dollars in sales within the next three years.

Hudson now has operations in Arkansas, Maryland, Indiana, Georgia, Alabama, Missouri, North Dakota and Kansas. He is keeping the headquarters at Rogers, where he and his wife have lived for more than 21 years. A new four-story office tower is in the planning stages.

Although the company could have its headquarters in any of the eight states in which it has facilities, Hudson has opted to stay where he is partly because it is such an agreeable home for his family. He also finds the business climate excellent.

"We don't have trouble getting people to move to Northwest Arkansas," Hudson says. "We do have trouble getting people to move out."

J. B. and Johnelle Hunt

Chairman and Treasurer / J.B. Hunt Transport Services, Inc. / Lowell, Arkansas

A dreamer and a doer since he was a boy, J.B. Hunt has been driven by ideas for making money. His enduring optimism, moderated by the steady caution of Johnelle Hunt, sustains him in the highly competitive world of trucking.

"We've been a good team," Hunt says of himself and Johnelle, who married him 35 years ago after his first business venture had flopped and he had a new job driving a truck.

Today, their stock in J.B. Hunt Transport Services, Inc., is worth about $350 million. They have seven terminals across the country servicing more than 2,000 trucks, and they employ more than 4,000 people.

For five years the company has been the most profitable one in its field. When Congress deregulated trucking in 1980 and many carriers went under in the new competitive climate, J.B. Hunt began a meteoric rise to national prominence with annual growth in revenues ranging from 31 to 55 per cent.

The Hunts are Cleburne County natives, children of the Great Depression. When J.B. was 12, he had to quit school and help feed his family.

While working at his uncle's sawmill as a teenager, Hunt first showed his penchant for innovation. When farmers came to the mill to buy wood shavings for poultry litter, they had to scoop them up from the ground. Hunt devised a raised bin to expedite loading and set about designing a machine to pack the shavings, a project which occupied much of his spare time for the next 15 years.

Johnelle was 16 and J.B. was 21 when they met, and she recalls helping him write letters about the packing machine. By that time, he had served an 18-month stint in the Army during World War II. Later he studied auctioneering at a school in Mason City, Iowa. He had been driving a truck and selling lumber for his uncle and thought he was ready to own a business. He and a cousin bought a livestock sale barn at Heber Springs and struggled through two profitless years, which left J.B. $3,000 in debt. A friend loaned him $10, and he hitchhiked to Little Rock, got a room at the YMCA and found a job driving a truck. Six months later he could afford a car and marriage to Johnelle, after dating her for four years. He was still designing the packer.

For the next 12 years, J.B. drove a truck, and he and Johnelle operated sideline businesses selling patio flagstone, cement and sod. J.B. excelled at generating ideas, putting together deals and making sales. Johnelle did the book work and collecting and often drove their delivery truck and laid sod.

On a run through Stuttgart, J.B. learned that rice millers considered rice hulls useless and burned them. He figured out that hulls made better litter than shavings. So he redesigned his machine to pack hulls, patented it, and, with Johnelle and a few stockholders, opened a rice-hull plant in Stuttgart in 1962. In 1983 they sold the plant at a nice profit.

In 1970, the Hunt Company bought a small refrigerated truck line in Kansas and moved it to Bentonville. Later, they got out of refrigerated trucks and into dry hauling and moved the headquarters to Lowell, where it is today.

After the move to Lowell in 1972, Johnelle resolved to become a housewife, figuring that she had worked long enough. They settled in their new home on Tuesday. The office called her to work on Thursday, and she has been there ever since.

Their son Bryan is the company's director of personnel. Jane, their daughter, is married to Dr. Jim Tinnin, a Fayetteville endodontist.

Hunt stock was offered publicly for the first time in 1983. By 1985, the company was ranked in the top 40 in the trucking industry.

Revenues in 1987 were 286.4 million.

Jerral W. Jones

President / Arkoma Exploration Company / Little Rock, Arkansas

Jerral W. (Jerry) Jones grew up in the Rose City area of North Little Rock, where his father, J.W. (Pat) Jones, owned Pat's Supermarket for many years. The younger Jones looks back fondly on those days around his father's business as the period when he learned the enduring value of the work ethic.

The lesson has served him well. Today, he is president and chief executive officer of Arkoma Exploration Company, which he founded, and has interests in banking, oil refining, real estate, insurance, shipping and manufacturing.

After graduation from North Little Rock High School, now Ole Main, Jones entered the University of Arkansas at Fayetteville, where he established a busy and varied lifestyle. He joined the Razorback football team, and, after his freshman year, he started selling insurance. By the time he completed his undergraduate studies in the spring of 1964, he had two thriving businesses and was married and had an infant son. He had earned a reputation as the "Businessman Razorback."

In the late summer of 1964, he faced a tough decision. Eligibility rules would allow him another season with the Razorbacks. Or, he could focus all of his energy on his family and business.

Jones chose to return

to the team, a decision he has never regretted, for it was in 1964 that the Razorbacks won the national championship. He was a starting guard and team co-captain. He says now that football taught him self-discipline, drive and team spirit.

"We were motivated by pride," he recalls. "It was a lesson in persistence, having a little bit of faith that if you're there and prepared, your time will come."

Football offered other benefits he has not forgotten. The Razorbacks traditionally have attracted a wide following among the leaders in business and government in Arkansas. Through his prominent role on the team, Jones was privileged to get acquainted with many Arkansans whose achievements he found inspiring.

One lasting relationship that grew out of his Razorback days was Jones' friendship with the late William E. (Bill) Darby, a well-known insurance executive who was attracted by Jones's enthusiasm for business as well as his skill on the playing field. This association enabled Jones to establish the financial base needed for his insurance business.

In 1969, Jones turned his attention to oil and gas exploration at a time when energy prices were stagnant and many were leaving the field. His timing was excellent.

He got into the business in time to be reasonably well established before the Arab Oil Embargo of 1973 touched off an era of soaring oil prices.

In the decade that followed, Jones steered a conservative course and resisted the temptation to plunge heavily into debt on the assumption that prices would continue to climb. Consequently, while many others have gone under in the depressed energy market of the 1980's, Jones has survived and remains well-positioned for the future.

While the field operations of Arkoma Exploration, his flagship company, are mainly outside the state, Jones has chosen to maintain his home and headquarters in Little Rock. He gives two basic reasons for this—his appreciation for the help and support of many Arkansans and his desire to offer his children the opportunities he feels are so abundant in the state.

Jones is active in many civic and charitable endeavors, among them the Boys Club and the YMCA. One of his favorite projects is the annual Red/White Charity Razorback Basketball Game, which benefits five Arkansas charitable organizations. Still an ardent sports enthusiast, he was honored in 1987 by being appointed state chairman of the United States Olympic Committee for the 1988 Olympic Games.

Jerry L. Maulden

President and Chief Executive Officer / Arkansas Power & Light Company / Little Rock, Arkansas

Jerry L. Maulden worked and studied for nearly nine years in night school to earn his college degree. During those years he was married and supporting a growing family. He had a goal of becoming an FBI agent.

He was awarded the degree in 1963 from the University of Arkansas at Little Rock, but upon learning that FBI service would require leaving the state, he decided to stay in Arkansas.

A CPA by profession, Maulden worked for a public accounting firm and later for Dillard Department Stores as controller. Maulden then joined Arkansas Power & Light Company as assistant to the treasurer in 1965.

On April 30, 1979, the AP&L Board of Directors elected Maulden president and chief executive officer, the position he still holds today.

His life has been shaped by tenacity and drive and willingness to work toward distant goals. He was one of only ten persons inducted in 1987 into the Horatio Alger Association of Distinguished Americans. The Association describes those it honors as "role models who give others a different kind of inspiration to succeed and ones who typify a determined spirit . . . and demonstrate that career success can be achieved despite a humble background."

Maulden was born in Van Buren County in 1936 in an era when money was scarce anywhere, but especially in the hill country of North Arkansas. His father worked for the Works Progress Administration—the WPA—a New Deal agency that was the employer of last resort during the Depression. When the WPA expired, the elder Maulden rode off with a few other men to North Little Rock to find work with the Missouri Pacific Railroad. He eventually made enough to bring his family to North Little Rock, where they lived around the poorer areas of town while Jerry attended public schools. His father died of leukemia in 1955, just about a year after he had seen his son graduated from what is now Ole Main High School.

A year later, Maulden met and married Sue Atkinson, daughter of another railroader. He credits her with being the most important force in his life during the struggle to get through college and launch a career.

After he settled in with AP&L, Maulden's rise through the ranks was dazzling. Promotions were frequent and significant, and he made it to the top in just 14 years.

During that time, he was away from AP&L only for about a year when he held executive positions with the parent company, Middle South Utilities, Inc., at New Orleans.

Maulden's civic work and the direction he has given to AP&L have won wide recognition for both the man and the company. AP&L received the "Arkansas Corporate Humanitarian of the Year Award" in 1983, the "Arkansas Conservation Organization of the Year Award" in 1984 and the "1985 Presidential Citation Award for Private Sector Initiatives."

Among the many honors awarded to Maulden have been the UALR "Shield of the Trojan Award," the "1982 Volunteer Industrial Developer of the Year Award" by the Industrial Developers of Arkansas, the "1985 Community Service Award" of the Arkansas Chamber of Commerce and the "Outstanding Service Award" given by the African Methodist Episcopal Church for his work in minority business development.

Maulden is a member of countless boards, among them the UALR Board of Visitors and the National Boards of Directors of the National Association for the Advancement of Colored People and the Boys Clubs of America.

He also has served as chairman of the Arkansas Industrial Development Commission, the Edison Electric Institute and the United Way of Pulaski County and has been president of the Greater Little Rock Chamber of Commerce.

Herbert H. McAdams II

Chairman of the Board / Union National Bank / Little Rock, Arkansas

Herbert H. McAdams II came down to Little Rock in 1970 and saved Union National Bank from near bankruptcy. At the invitation of a group of minority stockholders, McAdams purchased more than half the stock in the beleaguered bank and took over its management.

A local newspaper breathed an editorial sigh of relief that help had come in the form of an experienced banker and a man of unsoiled reputation.

McAdams restored the bank's financial integrity and good reputation. Union is now Little Rock's third largest bank.

McAdams has come a long way since the Depression, when, ironically, a bank failure nearly kept him from his dream of attending Northwestern University at Evanston, Illinois. The bank closed in 1930, taking with it all the cash reserves of McAdams's father, a Jonesboro surgeon. When young Herbert finished high school in 1933, the elder McAdams told him to stay home and enroll at Arkansas State College.

Undaunted, McAdams took $50 he had saved, hitched a ride to Chicago and strode optimistically into the Northwestern dean's office. He had applied earlier for a scholarship and told the dean he was wondering when he was going to get it.

"Today," the dean said.

McAdams took five part-time jobs and went on to earn his bachelor's degree, then won a scholarship to Northwestern's Law School. By then, Dr. McAdams's fortunes had improved, and he insisted that his son attend Harvard University Law School at the doctor's expense. McAdams obliged, but before the year was out, he had lost his father's support again—this time because he got married against his parents' wishes. He spent the next year in night classes at Loyola University at Chicago while working days sweeping floors. Then the doctor came calling again, this time promising a blank check for his son to transfer to the University of Arkansas Law School at Fayetteville. So McAdams came back, and by 1940 he was in the private practice of law at Jonesboro. He made $35 his first three months in business.

By 1943, McAdams was a deputy prosecuting attorney, a federal magistrate and city attorney for several small towns. He walked away from this to join the Navy. He ended up in 1944 on a ship awaiting the great Battle of Iwo Jima.

A surprise Japanese Kamikazee attack the night before the invasion left him burned over 60 per cent of his body and doomed him to more than a year and a half in the hospital and years more of chronic pain.

He came back to Arkansas, picked up his law practice, won a position on the Jonesboro School Board in 1948 (on a campaign to double the school tax) and organized his first bank in 1950.

Over the next 20 years, before he came to Little Rock, McAdams was a leader in school improvement at Jonesboro, organized industrial-development efforts in Northeast Arkansas and waged a personal campaign to bring out-of-state businesses to the area. He also acquired the Bank of Nettleton, Security Bank of Paragould and Citizens Bank of Jonesboro. He was a prime mover in the successful effort to win university status for Arkansas State College.

In Little Rock, he has continued his work in industrial development and higher education and has led drives for civic projects like the addition of a 7,000-square-foot gallery at the Arkansas Arts Center.

McAdams gave up law practice years ago, but, though now 73 years old, he continues to work in banking and public service.

Dr. George K. Mitchell

President and Chief Executive Officer / Arkansas Blue Cross and Blue Shield / Little Rock, Arkansas

Arkansas Blue Cross and Blue Shield touches the lives of nearly one out of every two Arkansans. The company privately insures 650,000 people and administers government programs covering another 300,000.

In years past, the public tended to regard the organization as an agent for doctors and hospitals to see that they got paid well for their services. The Blue Cross board, after all, had a membership of six physicians, six hospital administrators and six public representatives.

Today, Arkansas Blue Cross and Blue Shield is at the forefront of the effort to contain rising health-care costs.

Dr. George K. Mitchell was one of those physician members before he became the organization's first full-time medical director in 1968. He got his chance to begin changing the public perception of Blue Cross and Blue Shield in 1975, when he was elected president and chief executive officer. One of his first acts was to convince the board to increase its membership to 25, with the seven additional members all coming from the public.

In January 1987, under Dr. Mitchell's leadership, the organization became a mutual insurance company—meaning its policyholders are its stockholders—and the new 15-member board includes only two physicians and two hospital administrators. The new by-laws permit but do not require any provider representation on the board.

In Dr. Mitchell's view, Blue Cross performs "a delicate balancing act between customer and provider," striving to assure quality health care at the lowest possible cost. That's not an easy task at a time when inflation in health-care costs continues to outstrip increases in other areas of the economy.

"We deal with two of the most precious possessions of mankind," Dr. Mitchell says, "that's their money and their health."

Improvements in medical technology and the discovery of more effective drugs will continue to drive up prices. Even after the tremendous investments required for research and development, long and costly periods of testing must follow during which expenses mount without any income to the developers. Hence, as long as society demands the best treatment medical science can produce, costs will rise.

The challenge to Blue Cross, in Dr. Mitchell's view, is "to modify the behavior of all parties to be more cost-efficient."

One of the ways Blue Cross is approaching this task is the development of what it calls Primary Care Networks, or PCN's. Under this plan, physicians in an area agree to provide services at a reduced cost to the members of participating insured groups. Individuals choose their primary physician from the participating doctors, but they can only get to a specialist on referral from this primary physician. A major aim of the program is to reduce unnecessary use of medical services and hospitalization. There are financial incentives for physicians to keep costs down.

About ten years ago, Blue Cross sponsored the development of a new health-education program for kindergarten through the eighth grade in 25 Arkansas school districts. Soon the program will be statewide. Now the company is developing its own employee wellness program, which Dr. Mitchell hopes to see transplanted eventually to its corporate customers.

The idea, of course, is sound: good health means lower health-care costs.

A native Arkansan, Dr. Mitchell earned his Bachelor of Science Degree at Hendrix College in Conway and his medical degree, with honors, from the University of Arkansas for Health Sciences. He is certified by the American Board of Internal Medicine and is a member of the American College of Physicians.

Dr. Bessie Boehm Moore

Educator / Little Rock, Arkansas

Dr. Bessie Boehm Moore started teaching in a one-room school at age 14 at St. James, Arkansas, in 1916. She had a tenth-grade education. Now 85, she remains an active advocate of economic education, libraries and other causes.

Reflecting in the summer of 1987 on the success of her long career, Dr. Moore said:

"I've had time to think, and I've had time to work on new ideas . . . I've been a goodwill ambassador, and everywhere I go, I talk about Arkansas."

Born at Owensboro, Kentucky, she came to Stone County at the age of 12. Her teaching career took her from there to Pulaski County and on to Pine Bluff in 1924 to become Jefferson County supervisor of education. During the Depression, she did pioneering work in early childhood education, and in 1939 she became elementary education supervisor in North Little Rock.

When her husband, Merlin, became ill in 1947, Dr. Moore joined him in their business, Moore's Cafeteria in Little Rock. After his death in 1958, she joined the state Education Department as supervisor of elementary education.

Before her retirement from the state in 1974, she served as Arkansas's first su-

pervisor of economic education and first coordinator of environmental education. She founded the Arkansas Council on Economic Education in 1962 and was its executive director from then until 1979.

Here are other highlights of her life:

*She was a member of the state Library Commission from 1941 to 1979 and was chairperson from 1949 to 1979, serving under nine governors.

*First appointed by President Richard M. Nixon in 1971 and reappointed by Nixon and Presidents Jimmy Carter and Ronald Reagan, with the appointments confirmed by the United States Senate, she is a member of the U.S. National Commission on Libraries and Information Science. She has been the elected vice chairperson since 1972.

*She was a member of the boards of directors of First National Bank (1971-1979) and Maumelle Land Development, Inc. (1973-1976).

*She was a leader in the establishment of the Ozark Folk Center at Mountain View, the only center of its kind in the nation, and is chairperson of the Ozark Folk Cultural Commission, which built the center and leases it to the state.

*In 1926, she organized the first county library in the state at Pine Bluff.

*In 1964, she led a group of distinguished Americans sent by President Lyndon B. Johnson to evaluate the impact of the Marshall Plan on German industries. The mission was initiated by President John F. Kennedy, who had selected Dr. Moore not long before his assasination in 1963.

*She is believed to be the only person ever to receive major honors four times from the University of Arkansas. In addition to being cited as a Distinguished Alumna, she was given honorary doctorates by the University at Fayetteville and Little Rock. The Board of Trustees named the economic education center at Fayetteville in her honor in 1978.

*Presently, Dr. Moore is leading a nationwide effort to promote better library services for the aging.

*In 1987 the National Women's Book Association chose her as one of 70 women who have "made a difference in books and reading." And the International Women's Writing Guild included her among 12 women designated "Artists of Life."

A 247-page biography of Dr. Moore was published in 1986. It quotes one of her admirers as saying:

"Life is exciting around Bessie Moore."

Don Munro

Chairman of the Board / Munro & Company, Inc. / Hot Springs National Park, Arkansas

Don Munro is a survivor. The seven footwear plants his company owns in Arkansas are holdouts in an industry that has been devastated by foreign competition.

Sixteen years ago, American shoe manufacturers dominated the domestic market with 80 per cent of the sales. Today more than half of those manufacturers are gone, and American-made footwear holds only 17 per cent of the market.

Munro & Company, Inc., of Hot Springs, Wynne, DeWitt, England, Clarendon, Mount Ida and Clarksville is one of the few remaining "pure" domestic manufacturers—meaning that Don Munro has not succumbed to the temptation to import some of his line. Munro & Company makes all its products in Arkansas.

Munro came to Arkansas in 1959 to establish a New Hampshire company's first southern plant on the shore of Lake Catherine at Hot Springs. He added plants at Wynne in 1965 and Mount Ida in 1968 as the Arkansas operations thrived under his leadership. In 1972, Munro bought the Arkansas division and made it Munro & Company. Since then, he has opened his other four plants.

While the flood of imports has bankrupted others, Munro has managed to hold on to about $70 million a year

in sales, but with no growth in recent years and a decline in profits.

"I'm not a bit discouraged," Munro says, explaining that he believes his company's "reputation for service and integrity of product" has kept it alive.

Two business decisions he has made in recent years underscore his optimism. In 1985, he decided to produce his own brand of shoes (Munro Shoes) for the first time in addition to the lines the company produces for chains like Sears, J.C. Penney, Edison Brothers, Thom McAn and Kinney. In 1986, when the Child Life shoe factory at Clarksville closed, Munro bought it, saved 250 jobs and kept the brand name alive.

Four of his plants are in farming areas, and many of the workers are farm wives, whose families have felt the sting of the national crisis in agriculture. His DeWitt and Clarendon plants had been closed by other shoe companies before he purchased and reopened them in 1978.

In all, Munro employs 2,300 workers, and he preaches and practices his belief that the future of the company and those jobs depends on a cooperative alliance between labor and management. He instituted a health and fitness program ten years ago, long before such efforts became widely fashionable, and keeps employ-

ees informed of industry developments, company matters and the activities of their fellow employees through a quarterly newsletter, "Footprints," and other means. He maintains an open-door policy between his office and his work force. Every employee has the right to take a complaint to anyone in management, including the man at the top.

While working to keep morale and productivity up in his plants, Munro has been a leader in national efforts to gain a measure of protection for his beleaguered industry. For three years as chairman of Footwear Industries of America, Munro worked on a petition to the International Trade Commission and lobbied Congress trying to implement a five-year rehabilitation plan that would limit imports during that time to 55 per cent of the United States market. This grace period would have allowed American manufacturers to modernize and take other steps to become more competitive. Although the ITC approved the petition, the Reagan Administration failed to act on it. This year Munro and other industry leaders are attempting to get Congress to limit imports to the 1986 level of 81 per cent of the market.

Munro continues to worry about the footwear industry but remains optimistic about his company.

Lloyd E. Peterson

Chairman of the Board / Peterson Industries, Inc. / Decatur, Arkansas

Lloyd E. Peterson almost became a major league baseball player, but he came back home to Decatur, Arkansas, a dying town in the late 1930's, and went into the chicken business.

Decatur didn't die, and what eventually became Peterson Industries earned an international reputation in the development of better chickens.

Today, at age 76, Peterson is chairman of the board of his company, which started out raising little flocks of about 500 chickens in 1939 and now processes more than 45 million broilers a year and is one of the leading international suppliers of breeding stock.

Peterson Industries has 1,100 employees in Arkansas, Missouri and Oklahoma and The Netherlands and is about to open a breeding operation in Georgia. The company sells breeding stock in 40 foreign countries. Besides its employees, Peterson has 260 independent contractors in the tri-state area raising broilers and another 40 contractors producing Peterson breeding stock.

To supply the needs of its contractors and the company's own breeding and growing houses, which cover 1 million square feet, Peterson has a feed mill producing 900 tons of feed per day and a liquefied-petroleum gas distributorship.

When Decatur couldn't get a discount store to locate there, Peterson started one himself, and today it is the hub of commercial activity in the little town of 1,100 inhabitants. The town was left without a bank in 1938, when its only bank closed its doors, a victim of the Great Depression. Peterson organized the Decatur State Bank in 1954, and today it has assets of $32 million. Since 1981, he has founded banks at Jay and Grove, Oklahoma.

When Peterson started out in 1939, he intended to be no more than a chicken farmer, raising his own birds for sale to somebody else to process. Early on, however, he developed a feel for the future of the industry and recognized two critical areas in which he later became an industry pioneer: vertical integration and poultry genetics.

In those early days, the industry was fragmented. Chicken farmers were on their own and took all the risks of a hard freeze or a devastating epidemic. There were companies specializing in breeding, others which owned feed mills or processing plants.

Peterson was in the vanguard of poultrymen who saw that the wave of the future was for companies to integrate vertically—that is, to get into the business at every level from feed milling and breeding to growing and processing.

"We did not integrate because we wanted to," Peterson says, "but because we had to to remain in the business. Most of us dealt directly with the independent farmer. In good years, the farmer could make good money on chickens. The next year, he might take a sizeable loss."

Airplanes have played an important role in the growth of Peterson Industries. From a single-engine Bonanza purchased in 1946, the company's fleet has grown to five airplanes, flying about 5,000 hours a year.

Early in his business experience, Peterson, who had no formal scientific education, began studying poultry genetics. In 1945, using his garage and his 16 chicken houses, he began his initial experiments in cross-breeding. By 1956, he was marketing the "Peterson Male," a superior parent line that had captured 30 per cent of the United States market by 1959. Today, the majority of the male parent stock in the nation comes from Peterson Industries. An improved female was offered beginning in 1984, and the company sells as many of these as it can produce.

Today, most of the major chicken producers buy at least part of their parent stock from Peterson.

Jackson T. Stephens

Chairman of the Board / Stephens Inc. / Little Rock, Arkansas

Jackson T. Stephens is chairman of Stephens Inc., of Little Rock, the flagship of a financial empire that reaches into investment banking, stocks and bonds, manufacturing, computer services, equipment leasing, insurance, international trade, banking and many other areas of the economy.

While the Stephens investments and other economic development efforts are international in scope, the company and its chairman have maintained a strong commitment to the improvement of business in Arkansas.

One of six children in a family that never had much money during his childhood, Stephens responded well to his parents' insistence on self-reliance, diligence and industry. His achievements have proved the worth of those timeless values.

Albert Jackson Stephens imbued his children with a relentless drive to improve their material circumstances. It is said that he used to tell them:

"Don't be ashamed of your poverty, and don't be proud of it. Just get rid of it as quick as you conveniently can."

In those days, poverty was the common lot of most of the farm families like the Stephenses and their neighbors in rural Grant County.

As a youngster, Stephens picked cotton and helped neighbors harvest their crops. By the time he was 15 years old, he was a hotel bellhop and a shoe-shine boy and was delivering telegrams in his spare time. These were all jobs in which earnings tended to increase with productivity and good service. Stephens saw that connection early and has not forgotten the lesson.

When Stephens was ready for high school, he managed to go to Columbia Military Academy, where he got his diploma in 1941. He came back home and enrolled at the University of Arkansas at Fayetteville, where he studied for two years before he won an appointment to the United States Naval Academy at Annapolis.

He earned a Bachelor of Science Degree at Annapolis, but because of poor eyesight, he was denied a Naval commission.

After graduation in 1946, Stephens came back to Arkansas to work for Stephens Inc., which was founded in 1933. He became president of the company in 1957.

Under his leadership Stephens Inc., became the largest bond house off Wall Street, a distinction it held until 1987, when it undertook some corporate restructuring which made a technical change in the company's national ranking.

Stephens gained national recognition when he received one of the 1980 Horatio Alger Awards, which are given to individuals who have risen to prominence from humble beginnings.

A former member of the Board of Directors of the Little Rock Boys Club and former co-chairman of Quapaw Area Council of the Boy Scouts of America, he has served as co-chairman of the St. Vincent Infirmary Development Fund.

Stephens has been a major contributor to the University of Arkansas, Baptist Medical Center, St. Vincent Infirmary, several charitable organizations and numerous private colleges. He was also a contributor and a leader in the drive to establish the Central Arkansas Radiation Therapy Institute, known as CARTI.

He is a former member of the Board of Directors of the Missouri Pacific Railroad, Burlington Northern, Inc., and Wal-Mart Stores, Inc.

From 1948 to 1958, Stephens was a member of the University of Arkansas Board of Trustees.

The University honored him in 1965 with its Distinguished Alumnus Citation and in 1985 awarded him an honorary Doctor of Laws Degree.

C.E. (Doc) Toland

Chairman of the Board and Chief Executive Officer / Affiliated Foods, Inc. / Little Rock, Arkansas

When C. E. (Doc) Toland went to work for a cooperative wholesale grocery warehouse in 1948, he was one of only four employees. The co-op, called Model Markets then, had only 20 members, all independent grocers in the Little Rock area.

Arkansas had about 130 wholesale grocery distributors in those days. Competition was fierce. The chain stores dominated and were growing. Just surviving was tough for the fledgling cooperative, which had been organized in 1944.

Toland, who had yearned to be a grocer since his boyhood days at College Hill, Arkansas, sensed that Model Markets had a future despite its modest beginnings. He showed great foresight. In fiscal 1987, as chairman of the board and chief executive officer, Toland presided over the sale of nearly $426 million worth of goods to 251 member stores, making his company the largest wholesale grocer in the state.

Now known as Affiliated Food Stores, Inc., the co-op started out buying box-car loads of soap for its members. Today, the Little Rock warehouse stocks more than 16,000 items and turns over a $20 million inventory every two or three weeks.

While the independent retail merchant has been vanishing in many sectors of the economy, Affiliated has made it possible for independent grocers to hold an impressive share of the market.

In 1957, the year Toland took charge, the co-op rebated $9,831 to its 38 member stores. Last year, the 251 members got back $7,291,750 in shared profits.

Originally, the co-op members joined mainly to get advertising monies from manufacturers that otherwise went only to the chain stores. At that time, a grocer had to use a number of suppliers to keep his shelves stocked.

As the concept of the modern supermarket developed, Affiliated kept pace by offering more than dry groceries. Over the years, the warehouse has added frozen foods, meat, produce, health and beauty aids, and dairy products. Today, any one of the more than 100 trucks operated by Affiliated can carry virtually everything a supermarket needs.

Under Toland's leadership, Affiliated has developed several ancillary services to members. The company has its own advertising staff, an art department, a print shop, an accounting service, a trading stamp company, an insurance agency and even a Small Business Investment Corporation that can loan an independent grocer up to $250,000 to get started. Affiliated offers a sophisticated computer system to members that will keep prices current and automatically send orders to the warehouse.

Since Toland took charge, he has moved Affiliated into the production of dairy products and soft drinks. The bottling operation at Winnsboro, Louisiana, turns out Shurfine and Faygo drinks for Affiliated members and bottles under other labels for several major chains. Gold Star Dairy at Little Rock, built and operated by Affiliated, is the state's largest and, Toland says, is the most modern dairy in the world. Gold Star runs seven days a week around the clock with just 47 employees.

Toland's wife is the former Oretha Thomas. During their 41 years of marriage, he says, "she has unquestionably been my strongest support and adviser."

A past president and current board member of the Arkansas Retail Grocers Association, Toland is also on the boards of the National Grocers Association, Arkansas Wholesale Grocers Association and Metropolitan National Bank. He serves on the Business Advisory Board of Harding University and is a deacon in the Baptist Church.

Toland is also a former chairman of the Board of Directors of the Shurfine Central Corporation of Chicago.

Sam M. Walton

Chairman / Wal-Mart Stores, Inc. / Bentonville, Arkansas

Sam M. Walton and his associates at Wal-Mart Stores, Inc., have built the nation's fastest growing retail chain in little more than a quarter of a century. The Wal-Mart people attribute their success to Arkansas ingenuity, principles based on the Golden Rule, creative communication and a commitment to excellence.

The formula has served the company well. Today, the discount chain comprises more than 1,100 Wal-Mart stores, 100 Sam's Wholesale Clubs, a smattering of Dot Drugs and Helen's Arts and Crafts and the first new "Hypermart USA" stores, a fully Americanized version of a European concept of one-stop shopping.

The stunning growth of Wal-Mart from a single store at Rogers, Arkansas, in 1962 to its present operations in 23 states is one of the most phenomenal stories in the history of modern merchandising.

Wal-Mart today employs more than 180,000 people. Sales for the year ended January 31, 1987, totaled $11,909,076,000, up from $8,451,489,000 the year before. Net profits for that year were $450,086,000. Sales for the year ending January 31, 1988, were expected to reach $16.5 billion.

The origins of the company can be traced back to 1945, when Sam and Helen Walton opened a 5 & 10 cent store in Newport, Arkansas, under a Ben Franklin franchise. Bud Walton, Sam's brother, opened his first dime store two years later in Versailles, Missouri.

In 1950, after Sam and Helen lost their lease in Newport, they settled in Bentonville, Arkansas, where they opened Walton's Five and Dime.

By 1962, Sam and Bud Walton had a successful chain of 15 Ben Franklin stores and had become fascinated with the idea of large, general merchandise stores selling at substantial discounts. The concept was not new, but their belief that such stores could thrive in small communities went against the conventional wisdom of the day. The only discount stores at that time were in large urban centers.

The first Wal-Mart Discount City at Rogers became the proving ground. After two years of testing, trying and reworking, a second store opened in Harrison, Arkansas. Other Wal-Marts following in those early years at Springdale, Siloam Springs, Conway, Fayetteville, North Little Rock, Morrilton and Mountain Home.

By 1970, Wal-Mart had demonstrated without reservation that the citizens of small communities would welcome the opportunity to purchase a broad range of merchandise at discount prices. The family-owned chain had by then compiled an impressive financial record that enabled it to issue 11 million shares in its first public offering of stock. Sales that year were $44 million.

Just two years later, with 41 stores, Wal-Mart had sales of $72 million and won approval for listing on the New York Stock Exchange. An investor who purchased only 100 shares of Wal-Mart stock that year and held on to them would now own 25,600 shares. The stock has split two-for-one eight times in the last 15 years, and by the end of 1987, there were 564 million shares outstanding.

The 100th store was opened at Bentonville, home of the company headquarters, in 1974. Wal-Mart opened its 1,000th store in 1987 and has gone over the 1,100-store mark in 1988.

Sales have grown at a staggering rate. By 1978, they had reached $600 million, and by the end of fiscal 1987, they were approaching $12 billion.

Wal-Mart has changed the nature of retailing in America and gained wide recognition for its management style.

From 1977 to 1985, *Forbes Magazine* ranked Wal-Mart as the retail industry leader in return on equity, return on capital, earnings growth, sales growth and profitability

By now you should be getting to know us. You have read about our people, the prominent and the not so prominent, whose combined efforts are urging Arkansas into the future with positive direction and constructive purpose. I hope you liked our story.

When I set out to gather the material for this book, I had my biases. I won't go into them here—except to say that I had the notion that some areas of Arkansas were almost certain to enjoy a bright future, while others were just as sure to die a slow economic death. My taste in environments clearly favored the mountains and the foothills, and I tended to let my affection for the uplands determine my outlook for all of the varied regions of Arkansas.

By the end of my travels working on this book, I had acquired, quite easily, a new and much more hopeful outlook for all of Arkansas. All across the state I found Arkansans looking to the future–realistically and energetically. There are scores of towns and communities whose stories could have been told here, places where citizens are recognizing that they share a common fate and can best play a role in determining that fate by concerted joint effort. I wish we could have introduced you to all of them.

If there is one thing that these communities share, it is a growing understanding of the fact that we cannot rest on the accomplishments of the past or even the most agreeable realities of the present.

That's why Dumas, one of the most progressive little towns in the Delta for at least a quarter of a century, just got through adopting a 20-year program for economic development.

That's why at Calico Rock, when the town was trying to buy an industrial park, teenagers got out and cleaned yards and hauled trash to help raise the money. And that's why an old man at Calico Rock who was years beyond retirement, was not a native of the area and had no family anywhere around there chose to donate an unsolicited $360 to the effort.

They were all looking to the future.

So were we when we selected a photograph to bring this book to a close. We could have chosen a mountain vista, a view down a quiet bayou, a sprawling factory or a little white church on Sunday morning. We settled on some school kids, eager and smiling.

I think we've come to realize in Arkansas that we must begin now to build their future.

—Tucker Steinmetz

For their roles in the publication of this book, special thanks are due at least five individuals—Governor Clinton; Kay Kelley Arnold, Director of the Department of Arkansas Heritage; Patricia A. Sanders, Kay's administrative assistant; and Ron Robinson and Jim Johnson of Cranford Johnson Robinson Associates.

Kay was the guiding hand behind the writing of this book, and Pat provided flawless attention to the complicated scheduling and correspondence involved in the project.

We also express our gratitude to countless other individuals who contributed to the success of the Sesquicentennial through generous donations of time, energy and money.

I am personally indebted to several others whose advice and counsel were invaluable to me during the writing of "Tell Me About Arkansas." They are Sam Taggart, Bob Lancaster, Roy Reed, Clarence Hall and my aunt, Bobbie Steinmetz.

And a few words on this page cannot convey adequately my appreciation for the assistance, support and encouragement offered throughout the writing of this book by my wife, Ann.

Finally, I dedicate my efforts in this project to our grandchildren, Kyndle Laurette Steinmetz and Lucas Allen Childress, part of the future of Arkansas.

Tucker Steinmetz
March 1988

Arkansas Sesquicentennial Celebration Commission
Nan Brown, Executive Director

Wesley Hitt grew up in North Little Rock and is a graduate of Northeast High School in that city. He attended photography school in Massachusetts. A commercial photographer, he has had his own business in Little Rock for five years.

Tucker Steinmetz, a former newspaper reporter, also grew up in North Little Rock and attended public schools there. A free-lance writer now, he has degrees from Hendrix College at Conway and the University of Arkansas at Little Rock.